Supporting mental wellbeing,
building emotional sustainability

STEPS TOWARDS
KINDNESS AND
ACCOUNTABILITY

The dance of healthier relationships

Amberley Meredith M.Sc.

Registered Psychologist with over 25 years
experience in mental health

© Amberley Meredith 2025

Print copy: ISBN: 978-1-7640628-6-2
E-book: ISBN: 978-1-7640628-7-9

All rights reserved.

No part of this publication may be reproduced, stored in a retrieval system, or transmitted in any form or by any means—electronic, mechanical, photocopying, recording, or otherwise—without the prior written permission of the copyright owner, except for brief quotations used for the purposes of review, commentary, or scholarly work, with appropriate acknowledgement.

This publication is not a substitute for professional mental health advice or treatment. Readers experiencing distress are encouraged to seek support from a qualified mental health professional.

Published in Australia.

Protected under the Copyright Act 1968 (Cth) and applicable international laws.

For permissions or inquiries, visit:

www.adaptablesustainablepsychology.com

Editors: Kerry Laidler and Timothy Baril
Front Cover Design: Britt Wilson

Also Available in the Adaptable Sustainable Psychology Collection:

Book 1: The Subtle Injury of Influence

Managing experiences, people and media that affect your mental health

Book 2: I'm Getting There

Overcoming emotional obstacles and hidden patterns that can block change

Book 3: Self-Improvement Burnout

When to start, when to stop

Book 4: Steps Towards Kindness and Accountability

The dance of healthier relationships

Dedication:

This series is dedicated to everyone who has survived: survived pain, survived trauma, survived disappointment.

Your stories are the true history of human culture, and an integral part of our evolution.

About the Author:

Amberley Meredith has worked in the field of mental health and wellbeing for over 25 years. Her professional journey began in 1995 as a volunteer in a UK-based drug and alcohol drop-in centre. She went on to complete a Bachelor of Science in Psychology and a Master of Science in Health Psychology in the United Kingdom.

Amberley has been registered as a psychologist in both Australia and New Zealand for over 20 years. Across her career, she has worked in diverse settings including acute mental health care and working as an authorised officer, held roles in community mental health services and on a children's acquired brain injury team, run a regional eating disorder liaison service, and worked with numerous multidisciplinary teams. She has continued to operate her own clinic in private practice across most of her career, specialising more in trauma and disability for the past decade. She has designed and facilitated trauma-informed retreats and created psycho-educational programs for community and corporate environments.

Drawing on over 60,000 hours of professional practice with individuals, couples, and groups, Amberley created this self-development series to share practical strategies derived from evidence-based psychological approaches. Her work integrates knowledge from a range of therapeutic frameworks and psychology principles.

Amberley is committed to making psychological knowledge accessible and meaningful. Her educational resources are designed to support reflection, insight, and the development of emotional wellbeing in an inclusive, relatable way. Amberley is continually inspired by what people can achieve when vulnerability is met with self-belief.

Adaptable Sustainable Psychology Disclaimer:

This content is intended for general educational and informational purposes only. It is not a substitute for professional psychological advice, diagnosis, or treatment. If you are experiencing distress or mental health concerns, please consult a registered psychologist or qualified healthcare provider.

The concepts and tools described in this series are based on psychological theory and practice but are not intended to represent or replace personalised therapeutic support. Outcomes may vary based on individual circumstances.

The exercises and questions provided are for educational and self-reflective purposes only. If at any point you feel distressed, overwhelmed, or emotionally unsettled while completing these exercises or responding to the questions, please seek support from a qualified mental health professional. This material is not a substitute for therapy or clinical intervention.

Amberley Meredith is a registered psychologist with the Australian Health Practitioner Regulation Agency (AHPRA). Her registration prohibits offering testimonials or making claims of guaranteed outcomes.

Contents

Welcome and namaste – the divine in me honours the divine in you . 1

1. The Collective Harmony of Growth 17
   Exercise: The Type of Relationship I Accept is. 26
   Pause—Reflect—Landscape 29
2. The Subtle Influence of Stress on Our Relationships 33
   Exercise: To Displace or Deflect? That is the Question. 45
   Pause—Reflect—Landscape 48
3. The Map is Not the Territory. 51
   Exercise: Assumptions and Expectations 63
   Pause—Reflect—Landscape 66
4. The Relativity of Responsibility 71
   Exercise: Where are you on the Responsibility Spectrum? . . 83
   Pause—Reflect—Landscape 86
5. The Power of Self-Trust. 89
   Exercise: Releasing and Forgiveness. 102
   Pause—Reflect—Landscape 104
6. Power and Relationships. 107
   Exercise: The Compliments and Gratitude Game 118
   Pause—Reflect—Landscape 120
7. Communion or Communication?. 125
   Exercise: Role Plays… Oh Yes! 133
   Pause—Reflect—Landscape 135

8. Self-Acceptance: Your Ally for Kinder Relationships..... 139
 Exercise: The Piece of Paper 149
 Pause—Reflect—Landscape 150
9. For a Reason, for a Season, for Life. 153
 Exercise: "Dear Me ...Revisited". 164
 Pause—Reflect—Landscape 166
10. Review of Insights into You. 169
 Exercise: Insights Gained into Yourself 174
11. Adaptable Sustainable Psychology: 177
Final Words 181
 Final Exercise: Where Your Insights Inform Your Vision . . 182
Acknowledgments - With Gratitude 184

Welcome and namaste– the divine in me recognises the divine in you ...

Relationships can be part of the quintessential joy of our human existence. But they can also be a source of pain and suffering, whether our heart gets broken, whether someone precious to us is lost forever or the person we trust most in the world hurts us in an inconceivable way. Navigating our relationships and finding our way to peaceful shores together can be challenging. In this rapid-fire and demanding world, it can, sadly, be all too easy to take for granted the people we care about and those who care for us. It can be all too easy to take out our bad mood on those we believe will always forgive us. It can be all too easy to give someone we feel empathy for every chance, only to be hurt again and again and again.

Mastering our relationships takes a healthy balance of caring for ourselves appropriately in terms of our wellbeing, having good self-esteem, knowing all our different and diverse identities, and feeling secure, comfortable and content to be ourselves. When these aspects are well managed, it may help to reduce dependence or pressure on others to do these things for us. By enabling kind awareness of our own and other people's vulnerabilities and creating the space to continually improve our ability to be compassionate and accountable communicators we may find the dance of relationships flows more smoothly and elevates our experiences.

After you have learned how to meet and manage your own needs, you can begin exploring how to build and manage healthier relationships. By caring better for yourself, you may find it easier to balance between what you want and what the other person seeks. If you're having difficulty managing your own issues, you could easily bring those issues into your relationships, potentially causing unnecessary conflict. This is why you have been working on yourself first, before tackling any relationship issues. **Self-mastery improves relationship potential.**

It is a fairly universal experience that most of us, at some point, will try to get our self-worth deficits met by others. This might be achieved through using strategies such as negative attention seeking, making others responsible for our happiness or wanting them to fix things that are not their responsibility. To prevent this—and avoid creating a new set of problems—we can first undertake some inner work: learn to feel good about being ourselves, build confidence in our capacity to heal wounds and become more resilient, and develop self-trust to care for ourselves. All of which may help us to healthily balance our needs against another's. After we have mastered this, we may feel less reliant on other people to make us feel good or fix our life for us, validate or heal us. We can self-care and may then have the space to offer care to others. This could take enormous pressure off the relationship, and we may then be freer to enjoy connecting and creating on a solid foundation of mutual co-operation.

Having worked through the Books 1–3 in the Adaptable Sustainable Psychology (ASP) collection, you hopefully have gained greater insight into how you can care well for yourself now and pro-actively support your future self. Thus, you may

Welcome and namaste–the divine in me recognises the divine in you.

be ready to invest time into understanding how you can manage your relationships well and explore how you might protect yourself from entering or remaining in unhealthy relationships. It is by being comfortable to be you, and keeping tabs on your behaviours or vulnerabilities that could cause you emotional discomfort and managing them with self-care that you may achieve this. If you don't have needs that you believe must be met by someone else and you are not dependent on someone to fulfil them, this leaves your mind with more space to check if someone is mistreating you, using you, or manipulating you. You are free to check if you are being drained from having to do everything for someone and assess if they're manipulating or abusing you. You have the capacity to see when to step in to support, care for, and help one another and when to encourage someone to look after themselves.

By developing a strong sense of accountability when it comes to taking care of ourselves, we can protect ourselves and the other person from having unreasonable demands placed on them when we seek to have them meet and look after our needs. We also protect ourselves from the times when other people are simply unable to look after us, due to their own circumstances or other issues requiring prioritisation. We may find we can reduce the risk of harm from those who might use our dependence on another person as an avenue for gaining and maintaining control.

If we neglect our psychological and emotional wounds or have been unable to work out how to care well for ourselves, we can unconsciously look to others to provide this. There may be no ill intent, just an overriding desire to feel better without due consideration of how this could impact the other person or put us at risk. Some of us may have done this without fully realising it, unconsciously looking to others to be responsible for our happiness, validation, security. This behaviour can drain the other person or damage the relationship if it is unrecognised, and when we are not actively managing it, it may leave us open to being manipulated and harmed.

Abusive people can seek to control and manipulate others and use someone's vulnerabilities to their advantage, with limited concern for how their behaviour could affect the other person. The abuser may also feel worthless, and this can lead them to find someone who is also insecure and struggling to feel good enough, and then the abuser may exploit that vulnerability, knowingly or unknowingly. They may initially develop rapport through the shared wound of insecurity, but then, in time, begin putting the other person down, criticising any failing—no matter how big or small—always comparing themselves favourably so they can feel better. Frightened people can do hurtful things to others to try to feel safer, and they can do this without care for the cost to anyone else. They may not be bothered that they are achieving their aims by being negative or cruel towards another person. Something worth considering is that insecurity, or having any kind of pain, trauma, or mental health issue is never an acceptable excuse to misuse or abuse anyone.

Abusive relationships may make us feel worthless, unhappy, and exhausted. They are best avoided. But, to see them coming or to be able to recognise if we are in one, it can be helpful to be clear about who we are, what works for us and what doesn't, to know what kind of relationship we thrive in and have the confidence to wait until we find a relationship that helps us feel content, safe, and respected. Once attraction kicks in and we are emotionally entangled, it can be very hard for us to see what is

Welcome and namaste—the divine in me recognises the divine in you.

in front of us and recognise when it is not the best fit for us and what might be causing us harm or could be a problem later.

Many of us have had the experience of watching someone we care about entering into an unhealthy relationship and trying to warn them, only to be met with disbelief, denial, or a desire to protect the person based on feeling sorry for their past experiences that are used as a reason for their harmful behaviour. If you begin a relationship when you are full of self-doubt, not feeling good enough or are in a space of self-loathing, it is possible the relationship may not go well. That isn't to say the relationship can't end up being positive or useful. By being mindful that you are not feeling internally stable, not quite comfortable being yourself, or not feeling fully confident, you can see where you could be vulnerable to exploitation or being unreasonable in your demands of the other person, and you can then manage this safely. Awareness of how you are feeling about yourself means you can apply extra safeguards to look after yourself and the other person.

The place from which we start any relationship matters, as does establishing what kind of relationship environment we thrive in, as this may help us cultivate healthier and happier relationships. Being clear on what kind of treatment we wish to receive from someone, as well as what we can give without risk of being depleted, being confident that we can be happy living our life with or without that person gives us choices and room to move. It is preferable to want them in our life, rather than need them. When we are not dependent on having them in our life, it is easier (note: easier, not necessarily easy) to let go of anything that becomes abusive or damaging. When our happiness depends on being in a certain relationship, we could convince ourselves that it's worth waiting for the person to change, so that they stop the abuse. This outcome is not assured and could cost us dearly whilst we wait.

This is not to say we don't need help and support from one another. One of the greatest joys in relationships can be found in emotionally supporting one another. We can all benefit from hearing a compliment, receiving some reassurance and, at times, receiving some emotional support or practical guidance. It's healthy and natural to help and support one another, to find ways to thrive together. This is one of those Goldilocks moments where we find that balance between supporting ourselves enough, and supporting others enough. Being mindful to seek that support in healthy, open, and conscious ways without too much dependence or independence, and establishing interdependence.

Interdependence is where we mutually balance our support for one another and encourage one another's individual pathways. By being conscious of what help we seek, and where our personal resources are, it means we can then work out what we can do ourselves and where we require help from others. In a relationship, it can help to stay mindful so that we don't swing to the extreme ends of the spectrum. Thinking 'I should never accept any help whatsoever; I must do it all alone' or 'I absolutely need someone to make me happy, and I cannot look after myself' is potentially unhelpful. At times, fairy tales and the media can create misperceptions about what love and relationships are supposed to be and do for us. Thinking someone will always ride in to save the day or be that perfect person all the time is mostly unrealistic.

Relationships may do better in the long term when all parties hold similar values and are in agreement of how to treat one another, and where everyone contributes actively and equally. To support this, it may help to deeply understand what your values are, especially with regard to how you wish to be treated by other people. Be clear about what constitutes a healthy relationship, and what kind of treatment this does or does not include. Be aware of what pain or wounds you have from other relationships that could be triggered and could therefore benefit from being actively managed. Be mindful that while these do not become someone else's responsibility to fix, seek people who understand your history and support your healing rather than activating or triggering you. Look for those who behave mindfully in consideration of what you have been through.

As you may already know, relationships are not always simple, but it is worth taking the time to identify what works for you and what does not. If you are looking for healthy long-term relationships, maybe lifetime ones, you want to make sure they are with people who are invested in helping and supporting you to be the best version of yourself. Just as you want to be with people who allow you to equally help them to be the best version of themselves. If you plan to commit your whole life to someone, it is worth investing time and energy into preparing yourself and feeling able to make clear, confident choices about what kind of relationship and person can suit you best. This next part of the work is entails reflecting on what kind of relationships you do well in, what you can do to be mindful of in terms of your behaviour, what kinds of treatment you won't accept and how to protect yourself, and how you can co-create healthy relationship management through clear and kind communication. Recognising that, as always, this may vary for each of us. Your decisions about what you accept and allow in relationships is something that is likely to be best made by yourself, you know you best.

We delve into who you are from a relationship perspective and give you the opportunity to assess whether your actions are creating the healthy, positive relationships you seek. Look into what might go awry and how you could adjust or improve it. Discover how to find the point where kindness guides you—giving enough to support others in becoming the best version of themselves while also ensuring you don't take responsibility for what they must manage. Explore ways to assess how the relationship workload is shared so support is reciprocated (even if in different forms), and focus on managing only what you're accountable for. The best partnerships are often those in which we empower each other to make the most of being ourselves.

We explore common pitfalls that negatively affect relationships, including how limiting your stress might reduce unnecessary pressure or minimise inappropriate relationship demands. Examining what kind of relationship can work well for you and identify any expectations or assumptions that you may have regarding relationships that might not be conducive to harmony and longevity. By assessing where you're sitting on the responsibility spectrum, you may be able to see if you are creating comfortable personal accountability that allows growth in your relationships or hold an overly-responsible, under-responsible or irresponsible perspective that limits either yourself or the other person. We tackle the difficult subject of releasing negative experiences and explore self-forgiveness to build self-trust and see if working on letting go of a difficult event could be of benefit to you, and help ease the intrusion of a painful past.

By examining how power plays out in relationships, we outline ways to help you find a balance that keeps kindness central for all parties. We look at how circular relationships can foster equality, rather than hierarchies that often diminish one party or the other. We differentiate between communing on a soulful level for intimacy and communicating information effectively, and we offer ways to refine your communication so you can strengthen your relationships. We explore what might block healthy expression and receptivity, focusing on the difference between how you are received and how you are perceived. We reflect on how cultivating self-acceptance can improve our relationship experiences and how gratitude, humility, and understanding and adjusting our intentions may help us with this. We learn to see past others' reactivity—as well as our own—so that, if we or others are hurt, the hurt can be addressed constructively. And, finally, we take some time to sit with how grief and loss affect our sense of self and the relationship we have with who we were, who we are, and who we wish to become, and we consider how other relationships can form part of the supportive fabric that holds us through these times.

We will spend time understanding how these two fundamental components of **accepting and acknowledging accountability** and **cultivating a capacity for kindness** towards ourselves and others, may help build healthier, happier, and more supportive relationships. The importance of learning and improving relationship skills does not diminish across our lives. You do not build a lifetime relationship in five minutes, a few months, or a few years. It quite literally takes a lifetime.

If you have read the other 3 Books in the ASP collection, you probably understand that each book builds on the preceding work. In the first Book you were led through the maze of influences that can guide who you are, identifying what works for you and what doesn't. Book 2 introduced self-compassion and strengthened this skill; you learned techniques and tools that can support lasting change and looked to refine your positive emotional coping strategies to become more sustainable. Book 3 brought you deeper into the world of mindfulness and self-acceptance, to aid you in knowing when to change, and when to be content being you.

All these insights you have gained can now follow you into these next steps, in building your unique, psychodiverse portfolio to help you support and manage your relationships well. As in the previous books, the chapters are designed to flow in sequence, so you can skip sections, but the overall recommendation is that you take one bit at a time, carry out each exercise, and then move on. You may find it helpful to read a chapter at a time, then take a long pause and spend some time reflecting on what you have read to increase your absorption of what is important or relevant to you. You may take your insights to your partner, family, therapist, or your friends. The more you talk about what you learn, so much the better, as it can aid in reinforcing change and growth.

The Voyage into You – Instructions for the Journey

We provide these guidelines in each of our books to help support you and remind you of how to get the most out of the material. This work is in no way meant to replace active therapy, nor is it prescribed to fix serious psychological problems that require the support and help of a trained professional.

There are many ways that you might use this work. You may be using it on your own or as a couple. You could be a professional therapist using it with a client. You might even choose to do it with a small group of friends, or make it part of your professional organisation's wellbeing program. Whichever way you pick, take your time with it. It's designed to help you run the marathon, not win the sprint. The skills taught here take a long time to develop. By that, we do mean years. If you are seeking the quick fix then, sadly, this is not going to meet that desire. The human brain may take a very long time to integrate new ways of being into an automatic habit, it requires extensive repetition and focus, but the pay offs from staying the course could be well worth the effort. **Patience, repetition and commitment need to be your companions.**

If you're someone who has been exposed to trauma, please be gentle and patient with yourself throughout the recovery journey. You may require professional support and help from qualified therapists to fully understand all the psychological, emotional, neurological and physiological impacts of trauma. Whilst the techniques discussed throughout this collection of books have relevance to anyone who has suffered trauma, due to the potentially serious impacts on the structures of the brain, mind and body, you are advised to seek additional professional help.

It is always wise to approach any therapeutic care you undertake with an attitude of being kind and gentle with yourself, knowing that extensive damage may require an extensive healing period, and just because one technique doesn't suit you, it doesn't mean there is not another pathway that might work better for you. consider approaching your healing with a commitment to finding a way to support yourself and learning to adapt with whatever has happened, mitigating and managing the impacts, whilst finding a way to open yourself up to the joys and pleasures in life that could also be available. The powerful impact of trauma or pain may be inescapable, but the strength of your capacity to overcome it can be altered.

Take a check-in each time you pick up this book,

pausing to ask yourself where your level of coping is at today. Remember, there may be areas that could be triggering and difficult. If you're feeling too busy, exhausted, or even a bit too overwhelmed, you may need to come back to it at another time. Keep doing this throughout each section, making sure you are in a receptive space to sit with what is being opened up for you. You might want to set yourself up with some quiet time. You will need pens or pencils to write with. You can write all over the book if you so wish; have fun writing in the margins! Repetition may support you in how you learn and integrate ideas and new behaviours. Reading this book once probably isn't going to lead to absorbing all the information or ideas you may find useful. Read it, reread it again, and then maybe reread again sometime later. Keep coming back to conversations about what you have read and the insights you may experience, both in your own mind and when talking with others. This may help support and reinforce your learning.

Self-development can be an interactive and two-way journey. Where it involves the intersections of other people's actions, thoughts, and feelings with our own. Whether they be positive or negative, and no matter where that interaction comes from, be it a person, the media, from a therapist, or even from a book, change may come from the place where we meet with someone else's ideas or views, and we consciously choose what might help us on our way to feeling better.

The exercises and questions given in these books are for educational and self-reflective purposes only. If at any point you feel distressed, overwhelmed, or emotionally unsettled while completing any of these exercises or reflecting on the questions asked, please seek support from a qualified mental health professional. This material is not a substitute for therapy or clinical intervention. The exercises are derived from a vast number of evidence-based therapies and wellbeing theories, including neuroscience, mindfulness, polyvagal theory, hope psychology, positive psychology, acceptance and commitment therapy, cognitive behavioural therapy, solution and emotion focused therapies, and psychology from a trauma-informed perspective.

The tools are likely to work differently for different kinds of people in different situations. Sometimes, a slight shift in the format works better for one person than another. There is no one kind of psychological or healing modality that fixes everything for everyone. But by working with a wide range of ideas, methods, and people, you may find the parts that resonate with you and adapt what does not. This is how you can build your psychodiversity for coping through life's challenges.

Many of the approaches discussed in this collection of books may have a more neurotypical focus but could be possibly modified to suit those coming from neurodivergent space. Remember, the information and techniques given are not about a prescription, but guidance to help you on your journey of finding what works for you and what supports you in feeling comfortable to be you. Play with the suggestions given, alter the exercises to work for you, however your brain interacts with the world, be it through a neurodivergent lens or a neurotypical one.

Alexithymia is a neuropsychological phenomenon, also known as emotional blindness, it is a personality trait that makes it difficult to experience, identify, understand, and express emotions. The term comes from Greek roots meaning "no words for emotions". Those who have alexithymia may find that they experience emotions through physical sensations, behaviours (including risk taking ones), as a somatic/bodily response (such as pain, tension, tingling) or in other unique ways, and they may find it helpful to learn to acknowledge these experiences in lieu of feeling their emotions.

If you have alexithymia, you can still work out what your signals and signs are that indicate you are having an emotional reaction or response, and you may be able to develop ways to respond to the experience. It may work for you to ameliorate emotional experiences with responses or cues such as massage, drumming, tapping, exercise, eating appropriately, or talking about the situation with a solution focused perspective. For example, if anger and hurt are expressed in risk taking behaviour such as driving too fast or wanting to hurt yourself, you could take up boxing and have a punching bag at home and when the urge to speed or hurt yourself arises divert yourself to the somewhat safer choice of using the punching bag. You could use an exercise bike to ride as fast as possible; you could run or walk as fast as possible or use a virtual reality game that requires you to fight. Anything that you feel may help you work through the emotion and safely process it.

Please also note, that as we use some guided imagery work in these books those with aphantasia, a cognitive phenomenon that describes the difficulty or inability to voluntarily create visual mental images, may need to look at pictures to help evoke the same connections or feelings.

Before you begin this journey, we invite you to please take a moment of stillness and a singular, deep breath. Bring yourself fully into this moment. Whenever you pick up this book, repeat this process so that you can check that you are ready to engage fully with what you are reading and get the most out of the material. Please remember, this book is not meant as a replacement for professional therapy. You can use it alongside a program of professional treatment or as part of your own personal growth.

1. The Collective Harmony of Growth

In this section you will be learning about:

→ Why is collective growth important and useful?
→ How can discomfort fuel growth potential?
→ What do you value in your relationships, and how do you wish to care for others and be cared for?

You will need:

✓ Openness and honesty about your behaviour in your relationships.
✓ Willingness to lean into some uncomfortable growth.
✓ A pen and piece of paper to undertake a written exercise.
✓ To be open to discussing your reactions, feelings, and ideas, either with yourself or others.

1. The Collective Harmony of Growth

"Between stimulus and response there is a space. In that space is our power to choose our response. In our response lies our growth and our freedom."
 Viktor E. Frankl

One of the challenges of self-development is that we could become too insular in our introspection, possibly to the detriment of others. Behaviours that start off as a healthy choice could become fatiguing, pressuring, or maybe leading us to be self-absorbed and even entitled. Self-development is about kindness and accountability—not only in how we relate to ourselves, but also in how we treat those around us. It's as much about collective development as it is about personal growth. When we don't maintain a broad consideration for those we share this world with, the development of the self could at times come at the cost of our community, which we may rely on at different points in our life. The 'I deserve' mentality that does not consider the negative consequences for others could mean that when we ask people to help, they might not be there for us. Throughout human history, it has always been clear that we achieve much more together. Growing alone is hard, and doing it with others can also be tough. Yet, the gains made from collective growth can be just as valuable as self-development.

If you have come this far through the Adaptable Sustainable Psychology (ASP) collection, you have probably already figured out that personal growth is not always an easy or smooth ride. It requires facing some challenging aspects of ourselves, our life, and those in it. But growth does not stop at insight. Growth becomes a complete cycle when we put our insights into action, share them with others, and keep practicing them. In this way, growth may transform into lasting change that can feel truly worthwhile.

Sometimes, others can help us grow by doing something we do not agree with, or by challenging how we act towards them. The converse can also be true also, in that others can hold us back from growth by taking opportunities for responsibility away from us or by sharing all the same views and ideas, because when we are always in agreement, we may not feel any change is required. People tend not to change unless they become uncomfortable. Think about when you are sitting in a nice, warm, cosy seat that perfectly supports your body. You do not have to move, right? But should you be in a seat that makes your back ache, or your legs feel out of place, then you adjust your position until you are comfortable. You might choose to leave the seat altogether rather than trying to find a comfortable position. We typically only grow once we become mentally and/or emotionally uncomfortable enough that we recognise something requires our attention. We might leave a situation that is not comfortable rather than face some uncomfortable personal growth that could be required to improve the situation. We may leave because there is no chance to become comfortable if the other person does not grow with us. A wise mentor assured me that, whilst there might be discomfort, growth is there on the other side when we allow it.

1. The Collective Harmony of Growth

Growth may come with risks and undoubtedly, at times, require you to be courageous and venture forth without necessarily knowing the outcome. If you can find someone brave enough to travel with you on the path of growth, and they allow themselves to be vulnerable with you, the depth of intimacy and connection you may build could be priceless. The strength your relationship can gain, and the resilience developed may just be the foundation that sees you both through whatever future tough times could be ahead. Consider this: instead of being fearful of discomfort and growth, instead of avoiding the challenges in your relationships, you **embrace any problems as opportunities** to build a deeper, more compassionate connection that can serve you both as you move forward together. This kind of collective growth can make a resilient, reliable, and kind community.

The metaphor of the seed growing into a flower has relevance in reflecting the path of growth. The seed starts its life encased in a shell it was given and will outgrow, not knowing what lies beyond it. Once free of the shell, the seed finds itself in the dark with no map or guide. It pushes forwards regardless, to see what the journey ahead may bring. There might be some wrong turns along the way, some dead ends, and the sourcing of new paths. It's likely to encounter a pest or two that the seed must overcome. Once at the surface, there might be stones to grow around or inclement weather to cope with. But by continuing to grow, the flower may find itself alongside other flowers, who, too, have made the arduous journey to blossom together, and the beauty of being and then sharing this beauty alongside others becomes the ultimate reward.

Developing the ability to be comfortable when we are uncomfortable can assist us when growth is called for, whether we are growing alone or alongside others. By resisting or fearing that discomfort, we may create anxiety for ourselves, which could eventually cause us to feel distressed. In a distressed state we may find it harder to be present for others, and we may become involved in arguments and fights due to our inattention or low resources. This could worsen our situation further and cause yet more discomfort. If we start from a position of strength and make it part of our relationship identity that we warmly welcome challenges in our relationships, seeing them as opportunities to build capacity and create longevity, we may lighten and improve our experience. This doesn't mean we will always like it or that it will be easy, but setting ourselves up in this positive mindset may help us through the challenges and help us achieve the most growth we can together.

It is probably fair to say that we don't think too much about the details of the kinds of relationships we would like in our lives. We all too often either fall into them or they occur spontaneously, with little time for consideration given to what would suit us right now and in the longer term. By taking the time to clarify what feels acceptable to us in a relationship and what does not, we start to form internal boundaries and standards that can guide us when encountering someone who is not going to be a good fit for us. It can be very disappointing to meet someone we think is a great match because we share the same interests and hobbies, only to find out their values and way of treating us do not line up. Once we have that insight into what works for us, it may be easier to start investigating these types of qualities from the outset of the relationship, and then instead of just basing attraction on looks and shared interests, we can dig deeper from the start, possibly saving time and minimising risks of being hurt. Working out what we

1. The Collective Harmony of Growth

are looking for in a relationship does not, of course, mean that we don't have to change or work on ourselves. Relationships rely on growth to support longevity. If we stagnate, we may separate. Issues we didn't know existed often surface only after time together or during particular challenges, and changing circumstances may require us to change as well. Knowing what works for us is an advantage—but not a substitute for growth.

A friend of mine, many years ago, said she felt ready for a relationship after doing a lot of introspective work. She met someone special, but soon ran into issues that she'd thought had been resolved, and some she had not foreseen. It may be helpful to remain aware that our inner work matters, but it's also important to recognise that when it comes to being in the reflective space of a relationship, it can all change in an instant. There's only so much growth that we can do alone. There comes a point when the mirror of another person facilitates us in seeing things that were previously hidden from us. In my friend's case, this was certainly what happened. Fortunately, because she had done the work on herself before entering the relationship, she was able to understand this. This enabled her to work with the gift her partner offered her of further evolving together, and developing a lasting, intimate relationship.

Some of our relationship and communication problems may stem from the parts of us that remain vulnerable, such as our self-esteem, not feeling we are good enough or past hurts from previous relationships that remain unresolved. These vulnerabilities could leave us open to misinterpreting people's actions or words or not having the ability to convey our intentions or identify other people's intentions clearly. Being tired, stressed or in pain can also affect our capacity for communication and relationship management. When our inner resources are low, we are more likely to deliver inconsiderate communication and are less able to manage our reactions that come from unhealed wounds to ascertain when we might be reacting disproportionately, taken advantage of, or hurt. Our resources can be depleted due to feeling we have already given too much away to others, and we believe we have nothing left to offer.

In the previous sections, we have been learning to manage our mind by identifying feelings, thought patterns, beliefs, and behaviours that cause us to feel distressed and unhappy. We have been learning to become more aware of when we add more to our emotional and cognitive load through unhelpful expectations, self-judgment, or negative criticism. We have become more aware of any wounds we have sustained and how we may be able to continue to care for them and heal. Through this section, we take a look at how to manage all this in the context of a relationship, to support better communication, develop tactics to help us depersonalise negative behaviour from others, seek skills that may help defuse verbal attacks, and look at how to put in appropriate boundaries with ourselves and others. This may then give us the ability to support the cultivation and maintenance of healthier, fun, and growth-supporting relationships. In this section, **your growth comes alongside other people.**

A solo piece of music can be beautiful and unique. It can allow you to slip into a space of creativity and wonderment. But a duo, a quartet, or a full orchestra can create deeper levels of sublime mystery to unravel and revel in. Treat your life as you treat music. Take time for yourself, for that solo virtuoso performance. Take time for an intimate duet with that special someone. Move in and out of quartets with friends and colleagues to create something bigger and better together. Be part

1. The Collective Harmony of Growth

of a collective consciousness with society in your symphonic role. Play your part towards the uplifting of all humankind by being a kind and accountable person with yourself and others.

Exercise: The Type of Relationship I Accept is...

This exercise is like the one you undertook in Book 1, where you mapped out how you perceive yourself and what you know about yourself. This time, you are working with what kind of relationship you accept and developing clarity on what can work for you and what is not going to be a good match for you. In doing this, you may find you can save both yourself and the other person time, and possibly from being hurt, by ascertaining early on if you align enough to have some kind of relationship, be it as a partner, friend, co-worker, or family member.

You will need a big piece of paper for this exercise, preferably at least A4 size. Do not negatively judge how much or how little you put down. If you are struggling, come back to the exercise a few hours or days later and try adding more components.

Focus on how a good relationship feels, and if you do not know how this feels, if you have not yet had one, do some research. Think about what you haven't liked in previous relationships, what has hurt you, what makes you feel unsafe, what makes you feel bad about yourself. Then, write down what would be the opposite of this, for example, being lied to made you feel worthless, so you may prefer someone who

1. The Collective Harmony of Growth

is honest with you. Being told off for forgetting things made you feel insignificant, so you want someone who can be kind, understanding, and considerate of how they say things.

Perhaps look around for people who are content in their relationships and ask them what it is about their relationship that makes it healthy and happy.

If this is very hard for you to capture and work with, consider seeing a professional therapist or talking it through with friends or family members you trust and feel safe with.

Copy the following diagram onto the piece of paper and answer the following questions, adding to your relationship map. Some ideas and examples are given for each question. Think about all kinds of relationships here, not just intimate ones, but also family, friendships, and professional relationships. Maybe do a separate circle for each type of relationship:

1. How do you like to be treated? *e.g., with kindness and care.*
2. How do you like to feel in a relationship? *e.g., safe, supported, and heard.*
3. What behaviour don't you accept? *e.g., being hit, called rude names.*
4. What are your deal breakers? *e.g., infidelity, being cruel, and any kind of violence.*
5. What values do you wish to share? *e.g., treating others respectfully and with kindness.*
6. How do you hope to overcome issues? *e.g., discussions, working on solutions together.*
7. What personality traits complement you and challenge you in positive ways? *e.g., calm, motivating, organising.*

8. What communication styles do you work well with? *e.g., direct, open and polite.*
9. What kinds of activities do you enjoy doing with others? *e.g. being in nature, exercising, travel.*

Example:

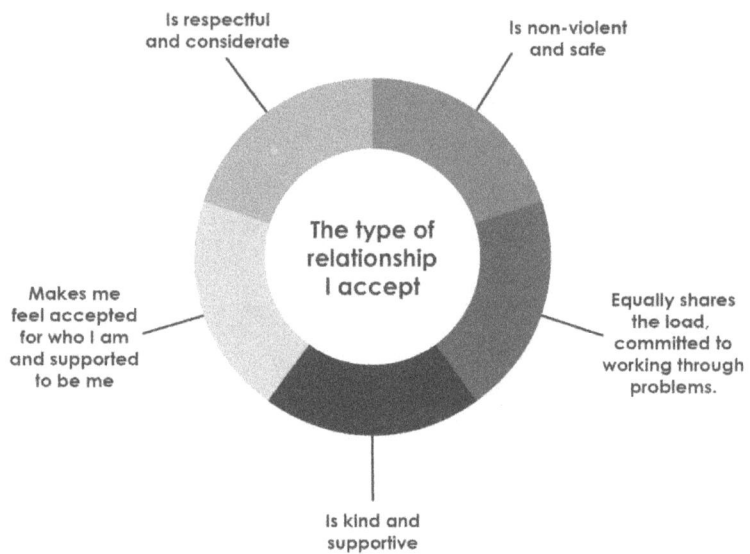

If you find this exercise brings up difficult emotions, please pause and consider seeking support from a therapist or mental health professional.

1. The Collective Harmony of Growth

Pause—Reflect—Landscape

We are working on developing our own Adaptable Sustainable Psychology, so we may learn how to help ourselves feel better, treat ourselves better and treat others better. At the end of each section, we want to reinforce and integrate any new knowledge. Reflecting on the material in relation to ourselves and our own life may help with this and, where relevant, show us where to adjust our behaviour accordingly.

1. Pause - Take a moment to sit with what you have just learned and consider it.

- Growing alone is only part of the work we do; we also learn how to positively grow together to create kinder, more collaborative, and safer communities.
- Growth comes with risks and challenges, but we can turn those into opportunities that may improve our lives and other people's lives.
- Taking time to consider what makes a good relationship for us can be supportive and we then may use this information to guide us in finding relationships that work well in all areas of our lives.
- We can find being mindful of and managing our past wounds, current stresses, and possibly unhelpful

behaviours when we are tired, activated or in pain reduces the extent to which these factors may negatively affect others and possibly damage our relationships.

2. Reflect - Answer the following questions:

- Are you someone who has invested a lot of time in thinking about what helps you feel good in a relationship? Is this something you feel comfortable exploring more?
- Have you had any good experiences of growing with another person, where a challenge came along and you worked together to fix it?
- Is there anything that might stop you from thinking about and asking for certain things in a relationship for you to feel safe and content?

3. Landscape - Step back from the details and see how this new information fits in with the bigger picture of your life. Consider your history, what is going on for you now, who and what is in your life, and the future you want for yourself.

- ✓ When you look back over your life, can you see times where you have been unable to change or improve a relationship? Why was this? Were either of you unable to engage in meaningful dialogue about the circumstances? Could one of you not get past what had happened or adjust your position to work together?
- ✓ What can you learn from these previous situations that could help you in your current and future relationships? What can you change about yourself that would help?

1. The Collective Harmony of Growth

What qualities or skills could the other person bring to help create a different and better outcome?

✓ If you are aware of some blocks that stop you from feeling safe to ask to be treated in certain ways in relationships, or fears that make you think you are not allowed to have standards, is there a supportive or therapeutic pathway available to change this and give you the comfort and confidence to ask others for what you need?

2. The Subtle Influence of Stress on Our Relationships

In this section you will be learning about:

→ What is good stress, what is bad stress, and why does knowing this help?

→ How managing limits on your stress can be helpful for your relationships.

→ What are displacement and deflection strategies, and how can you use them to navigate your stress limits?

You will need:

✓ Any prior insights you have noted down from Books 1–3 about your beliefs and how you cope.

✓ A pen and paper, and time to complete an exercise.

✓ If available to you, someone you trust to do the exercise with (partner, friend, therapist).

✓ To be open to discussing your reactions, feelings, and ideas, either with yourself or others.

2. The Subtle Influence of Stress on Our Relationships

"The greatest weapon against stress is our ability to choose one thought over another."
William James

One of the reasons we talk so much about stress in our modern society is because of how toxic and damaging it can become to us. Too little stress and we can feel deflated, depressed, unmotivated and lethargic. Too much stress and we can become tired, physically unwell, mentally overwhelmed and burnt out. But stress doesn't just have a direct impact on our mental and physical wellbeing, it can also subtly influence and negatively affect our relationships.

There are two types of stress we experience. There is the type that helps us feel motivated, engaged, and present; it's called eustress and is the good type of stress. Then there is the bad type that makes us feel overwhelmed, anxious, pressured and physically sick; this is distress. Stress can be stimulated through both our internal and external environments. Our internal experience of life may generate stress via our thoughts and beliefs, how we see something, and how we choose to engage with it. Externally, events, other people's behaviour, and their expectations may also drive our stress. We cannot always control or influence externally generated stressors, but we can learn how to manage our internal interactions with stress, and whether we manifest ourselves into a state of distress. This may be easier when we understand how we add to our stress—by taking on too much and through our perceptions of ourselves and our situations—which, handily, means we can proactively manage and limit it.

Once our internal experience of stress is under our control, it is usually easier to identify options available to manage our external stress. Managing the limits on how stress affects us and the ways in which we then interact with others as a result forms another thread in the tapestry of our psychodiversity. Being able to acquire the tools to proactively manage stress allows us to adapt in accordance with both our internal and external environments and seek the optimum conditions that could help create sustainability and protect our relationships. Should stressors last over protracted periods of time, they may require continuing care. Forewarned is forearmed. Identifying stressful areas of our life, the people or types of people that can make us feel stressed, gives us the opportunity to make different choices around how we perceive and engage with these things. The ability to manage stress well is a skill worth honing.

So, how do you know when you are under too much stress? Do you wait until you are burnt out and physically in a heap? Or are there other ways to check-in and limit those stressors before you become too stressed? Working out how to support yourself before a breaking point is reached is part of developing an Adaptable Sustainable Psychology. Remember, you know yourself best. Maybe start by asking yourself the following:

2. The Subtle Influence of Stress on Our Relationships

- What are my signs that I am beginning to fray at the edges and taking on too much?
- Do I start to get excessively tired?
- Do I forget simple, everyday things?
- Do I become snappier with other people?
- Do I withdraw and isolate more to avoid being drained by others?
- Does my alcohol or drug intake increase?
- Do I have stressful people around me right now?

One way to answer these questions could be to use your regular, weekly self-check-in exercise from Book 3 and ask yourself if you're taking on too much. Once you have established a clearer idea of what and who makes you feel stressed, and you know the signs that suggest you are becoming overwhelmed, you can start to employ stress management techniques. Dr Wilson, in his article *Self-Limiting Your Stress (July, 2023)* suggests two techniques that could alleviate the pressure of too much stress. You can **displace the stress**, this means you find a way to lighten your load by seeking help, for example, this might come in the form of delegating some tasks to other people. Or you can **deflect the stress**; this means you delay some tasks to reduce the amount you have to deal with at once, e.g., putting off some tasks until you have more energy, time, resources, and flexibility to undertake them.

For example, you want to have a child whilst you are studying and trying to work at the same time. To remedy the situation, you could forgo the study until your child requires less care, a deflection strategy. Or you could arrange for your child to be cared for by another family member, a displacement strategy. In both these examples, we see steps being taken to self-limit the stress to avoid reaching a breaking point and still achieving the goal. It may take a bit longer, but at least you get there and may not break along the way.

When considering how we manage our stress, it can be helpful to acknowledge the possibility that we may have blind spots. We can all have them. Our minds are impressive; they can convince us of all sorts of things, including telling us that we are coping, and can take on more, when we really can't. The mind can ignore the reality of how the brain and body are managing. We may be struggling to keep up with the current load, let alone do more. To better manage your blind spots, you could use the self-knowledge gained from the earlier work in Books 1-3 and identify what your typical patterns of behaviour are when it comes to managing stress, then apply self-care and protective measures to keep on top of your stress limits. Come back to what you know about yourself.

- Are you someone who can push to get ahead? Can you be too demanding of yourself?
- Do you take on too much? Do you struggle to say no?
- Do you fall into the perfectionism trap? Or do you have high expectations of yourself?
- Do you overly invest in caring how others perceive your efforts?

Managing your threshold for stress is your responsibility, and the power to do this comes from your perceptions and your choices. But managing stress isn't always clear-cut and this is why we have left this section until now. After doing the work from the previous Books, you may now know yourself

2. The Subtle Influence of Stress on Our Relationships

better and be able to recognise underlying fears or beliefs that might be driving you into stressful situations. You may have access to tools to actively manage these fears, be able to adjust unhelpful beliefs, and use healthy coping mechanisms to support yourself through difficult times. This kind of information could help support you in how you manage stressful situations. For example, you fear saying no to your boss in case you lose your job, so you take on more work and risk becoming sick from the stress of it. This could cost you your job any way, and you may then end up too sick to do any work. Having identified that this work is overwhelming and the fearful relationship with your boss is unsustainable, you might attempt to use deflection as a strategy. You could negotiate better working conditions from a space of believing you are being fair and reasonable, and that you a valuable employee. Or you could use a displacement tool if your boss refuses or is not approachable. You accept that whilst you might not instantly be able to change your situation, there may be other solutions. As you have started to cultivate your capacity for patience, increase your self-worth, and become more committed to finding the best for yourself, the idea of seeking alternative employment and then quitting your overly demanding boss might feel more achievable. Either way, deflected or displaced, you have managed your stress and used self-knowledge and sustainable coping methods to support yourself through the difficulty.

A trap many of us may fall into is not being good at saying no and therefore continually taking on too much. This pattern is seen predominantly in people who are overly-responsible, perfectionistic, or people pleasers, or who find boundary setting challenging. This might be a good time to ask yourself how good you are at actually saying no? We eternally seek the balance of having enough of the good stress to remain motivated and the reduction of any distress that makes us feel bad and which could, if unmanaged, make us sick. By being aware and actively looking at what causes you to feel distressed, knowing the warning signs that there is too much bad stress in your life, and using a pre-developed plan of how to manage stress, you may then be able to limit its impacts. Thus, you can take proactive steps, so that you don't take on more than you can manage and it might be easier to say no to others.

Why Maintaining Your Stress Awareness is Important in Relationships

It is an intricate process, finding enough healthy stress to remain motivated, engaged, and productive, whilst managing the reduction or elimination of worry, fear, and depression. But by working on maintaining this delicate balance, we may find it is easier to live in a state of collective responsibility with one another, where we have space to nurture those around us because we have the emotional and cognitive bandwidth available, and the time and energy to do so. The subtle influence of stress on relationships can profoundly affect the quality of our connections and how we experience others.

Let's take a look at what can happen to our relationships when we are not managing our threshold for stress, and we start to tip into distress. A lack of personal resources can mean our discussions turn into unhelpful arguments with one another. When someone is under too much stress and caught up in anxiety and fear, they often can only see their own distress. If someone feels they have no care left after giving so much to their job, children, or friends, they may shut down.

2. The Subtle Influence of Stress on Our Relationships

Someone could be in so much pain they cannot focus on anyone or anything else. All these situations can deplete our resources and may result in a feeling of having nothing left to give. So, when that one extra person comes looking for something from us, and it could be small or innocuous like an opinion or something bigger like taking on a project, we may respond in a defensive way that leads to heated arguments and hurt feelings. Not managing our stress can leave us too short on energy to communicate that we have nothing left to give at times.

If you have ever ridden a motorbike and dropped it, you may know that it does not matter how strong you are, there comes a point where the motorbike cannot be held, and it will fall over because gravity wins. The bike must be released to the ground and then picked up. For those of you who have not ridden a motorbike, another example would be placing a book down on the edge of the table, it can overhang by a certain amount before the tipping point is reached, and then it will fall to the floor. Our emotions and hormones can function in a similar way. Once you reach a certain emotional tipping point, with too much stress and move into distress, your body is cued to release all the relevant hormones to accompany this feeling. Once the hormones are released, it may take some time before we can return to a calmer and less activated state.

The idea is to train ourselves to intervene before we reach that tipping point whenever possible. By putting the ambulance at the top of the cliff, we manage our emotions before they put our body into overwhelm, and we end up with too much adrenaline and cortisol in our system and we cannot think or act clearly. Thus, instead of ending up in the fight-flight-freeze state, where anxiety or fear may affect our decisions, we remain more capable of making a calm, conscious choice, by sitting in a compassionate and balanced place of reason. This means we may have something left to give to our relationships. Even if it's only a gentle refusal to take on anything more, we can do it with kindness and a clear explanation, rather than dropping into anger or ignoring people.

Our lives are made up of relationships of all kinds. Even people who don't want to label their connection with another person as a relationship are still in relationships. The moment that you are connecting with and relating to another person, you are in a relationship. It might be a brief relationship of a few seconds, such as a chat with a checkout clerk, or an ongoing professional relationship with your doctor. Or it could be an animal relationship with your cat or dog. Or it could be the 30-year relationship with your best friend. There are no escaping relationships, our lives are full of them. Therefore, looking after them would seem to be sensible.

Given that relationships are everywhere in our lives, we give them surprisingly little forethought, planning, or preparation. We often are simply of the mindset that we just want one or we just get on with having them. This has the potential to cause us problems, especially if we are also not managing our threshold for stress, as we might move into being unfair, overly demanding, or dismissive of what others might need from us or being around people who can't see our stress and try to take more from us. Investing time into thinking about the kind of relationships we wish to have, how they might feel, and how we would like to treat one another, gives us a scaffold to start building healthier connections. When we know what each other wants and needs, we can then assess this against our capacity and adjust our stress levels accordingly.

2. The Subtle Influence of Stress on Our Relationships

For many, a connection with another person is highly significant. It is one of the basic drivers of being human and at times we may feel compelled to seek connections out, in one form or another, throughout our lives. Whether we are connecting to one or many, we sometimes feel better from being with another person who can help us feel seen and understood. We have been bathed in a plethora of stories, written across history and in the modern world, about love and everyone trying to define what it might be, how you might best get it, and how you might best hang onto it. Some of this may be immensely useful, and some of it might not be so helpful. A familiar behaviour we can pick up is offloading our stress onto others—sometimes because we assume their love comes with automatic forgiveness. Or we might believe that it is their role to be an emotional drop zone for us; parents could often foot the bill for this one. We can think our relationship threshold is strong enough to support additional stress, without giving it proper due care and attention to check that it always is. So, instead of self-managing our stress, we project or transfer it, possibly onto someone who does not have the capacity to hold this energy for us. This strains the relationship and may put it at risk from overload. One person cannot be everything all the time, and sometimes Prince or Princess Charming can't save the day, despite what the fairy tales might say.

Collective harmony is born out of recognition, appreciation, and collaboration. We need to be seen by others, but also to see others. We need to feel appreciated but also show our appreciation of others. We need to do some things alone and some things together. We all need someone at some point. But an overreliance on that support person, without considering where they might be in their own life, is maybe not a healthy dynamic for you both and the relationship. It may help to think about our relationships, prepare for them, and manage our own stress well. Otherwise, the relationship could breach its threshold and potentially break. If we are self-limiting our stress first before asking others for their support, we may find we are in a clearer space and can then see who can provide us with help and who is maybe buckling under their own pressures.

Self-limiting your stress is not just about you. It is about the honest recognition of how you manage stress in the context of any relationship. Just because your day is intense and demanding, would that make it ok to be rude to the cashier at the check-out? Does it mean that your partner at home must listen to you vent, after having had a difficult day themselves? Is hitting your child, partner, or parent ever acceptable because you feel distressed? Of course, none of these things are OK. If you learn to self-limit your stress, then you significantly increase your chances of creating harmonious, loving, and respectful relationships.

This Book is going to help you to explore any triggers that could tip the relationship past its threshold. Seeking out the vulnerabilities that might adversely affect your connections with others and work out strategies that may enable you to manage your internal stress to help lessen any negative effect on your relationships. Having worked out how to be kind and accountable with ourselves, we may then commence working out how to be a kind and accountable person with others, and from here we may grow into a space of collective harmony and share in the collective joy of working together to create a more peaceful existence for everyone.

Exercise: To Displace or Deflect? That is the Question.

This exercise can help you work out if you can use either deflection or displacement strategies to proactively manage your stress, so it does not subtly impact your relationships as much, or help you to identify if there might be any blocks to you using them.

1. First, pick a recently stressful situation or even a current one, and then answer the following questions to ascertain whether the stressful situation can be deflected or displaced.

Displacement:

- What am I responsible for in this situation?
- What, if anything, is the responsibility of other people?
- What could I ask for help with? Certain tasks, positive encouragement, or extra emotional support?
- What could I let go of elsewhere in my life to lighten my load?

Deflection:

- Can any of my goalposts be moved or plans changed?

- Do I have expectations that could be changed or softened?
- Does everything I want to do have to be done at the same time?
- Are there things that could be delayed or given to other people to look after?

2. Looking at your answers to these questions, and either working by yourself or with a trusted person, identify if there are any potential obstacles to implementing these ideas to self-limit your stress. Look over your work from previous sections to see what you have learned about yourself so far, and use the following questions to check for support and identify any blocks to change.

→ What are my strengths? Can I use these to help support me in deflecting or displacing my stress?
- *E.g. I am persistent and good at helping others. I could help myself by pretending I am helping someone else and not give up until a suitable solution has been found.*

→ What attitudes, expectations, or behaviours might cause me a problem when using the deflection or displacement mechanisms to self-limit my stress?
- *E.g. I am insecure at times and sometimes feel I need to prove myself. This means I can take on too much, and don't share the load, to my own detriment.*

→ Is it possible I have a perfectionist tendency, or that I am stubborn, or do not ask for help? Can I say no to protect myself? Do I lack personal agency and don't believe that I can influence my life through my actions?

2. The Subtle Influence of Stress on Our Relationships

- *E.g. I feel responsible for others and want to help, and whilst I am compassionate for others, I am less compassionate for my own limits. I can be a perfectionist with some things and then overwork the details. I find it hard to make choices that help me.*

→ What can I do about managing any obstacles that I have identified?

- *E.g. I can use regular self-check-ins to be more mindful about where I can come undone. I can talk to friends about my warning signs of when I am under too much stress and ask them to gently remind me to help myself before it is too late.*

→ How can I use what I have learned so far to overcome challenges to be better able to take care of my own stress and therefore have more resources available for both myself and others?

- *E.g. I can use the brain retraining exercises to help change past patterns of saying "yes" all the time and improve my self-worth. I can practice self-compassion and mindfulness exercises to better identify when my brain and body have enough going on. I can support myself by talking more encouragingly in my mind about managing stress better.*

If you find this exercise brings up difficult emotions, please pause and consider seeking support from a therapist or mental health professional.

Pause—Reflect—Landscape

1. **Pause** - Take a moment to sit with what you have just learned and consider it.

- Excess stress can be damaging physically, mentally, and emotionally, and it could harm our relationships.
- Stress comes in two types, both good and bad, one can help us and the other may harm us.
- Stress can be generated by us taking on too much, how we see situations or talk to ourselves, and by the events and situations that are happening to us or around us.
- Understanding and thinking about how stress can negatively impact our relationships is important. We can hurt others or push them away when we are not managing our stress, potentially hurting ourselves as well should we lose that relationship.
- If we are not limiting our stress levels well by using our self-knowledge to manage exposure and change how we are thinking about ourselves and situations, we could risk negatively affecting our relationships.
- We can deflect or displace stress by either engaging help and delegating or delaying what we are undertaking.

2. The Subtle Influence of Stress on Our Relationships

- We can inadvertently take our stress out on others when we are not managing it well, making saying no and not taking on too much a protective measure, to ensure our resources are maintained and managed sufficiently to be able to continue to care for our relationships.

2. **Reflect** - Answer the following questions:

- How do you think you manage stress currently? Have you got a tendency to take on too much and if so, where does this come from: a need to prove yourself, a feeling of responsibility or fear of not doing or being enough?
- Can you see how stress affects your current relationships? Do you see people being more careless and less considerate when they are stressed? Do you see them running out of steam and having less energy to put into relationships?

3. **Landscape** - Step back from the details and see how this new information fits in with the bigger picture of your life. Consider your history, what is going on for you now, who and what is in your life, and the future you want for yourself.

- ✓ Looking over your life, when have you experienced either being too stressed to look after a relationship or been in a relationship where the other person was too stressed to look after the relationship?
- ✓ What can you learn from these experiences that you can take charge of and change? Are there underlying issues, like low self-esteem, previous damaging or traumatic experiences, or how you seek approval or build self-worth? Would any of these benefit from being addressed to help reduce your stress load more effectively and therefore support you in caretaking your relationships better?

3. The Map is Not the Territory

In this section you will be learning about:

→ Where do our relationship maps come from—and why don't they always take us where we want to go?

→ Why do we develop unconscious expectations about relationships?

→ How expectations feed assumptions and can create unnecessary tension and disappointment.

→ Why we assume people we're in relationships with will behave the same way we do.

You will need:

✓ An honest awareness of your current self-esteem.

✓ An attitude of self-compassion for the things you recognise are not so great about your past or current behaviour.

✓ A pen, paper, and possibly a trusted friend, partner, or therapist, to carry out a reflective and written exercise.

✓ To be open to discussing your reactions, feelings, and ideas, either with yourself.

3. The Map is Not the Territory

"Assumptions are the termites of relationships."
Henry Winkler

If we are to look after ourselves and look after our relationships, it may help to understand how and why they might become damaged, broken, or dysfunctional. The battle for power and control is one of the issues that can cause conflict in our relationships. This might be because we can, at times, feel as though we have little to no control in some areas of our lives, and this powerlessness can feel uncomfortable. This, in turn, can lead us to seek out power where we can. A relationship may be the easiest space in which to achieve this. Power over another person is a chance to direct and control things. Of course, with two people (or more) vying for power, this can get explosive and difficult. It can create tensions and problems; people don't like to be controlled or feel powerless. If power becomes the focus, both accountability and kindness might go out the window in the bid to feel in control.

We have begun to rely so much on virtual communication through mobiles, texting, chat rooms, AI chatbots, posting on platforms that we may find we are at risk of losing a significant portion of our ability to engage in real-life conversations.

From repeated exposure, we can become conditioned and so well-rehearsed at recording vlogs, making social media videos, or leaving voice messages, it can minimise our conversational skills. When talking with people in real-time, it can sometimes end up feeling like we are listening to a monologue. They focus on telling us about their knowledge, their experiences or their opinions. There is no back-and-forth or exchange, no active engagement in our responses, leaving us feeling more like a member of the audience than a participant in a dialogue. There are now so many online opportunities for us to become experts, offering uninformed or partially informed opinions, at times without sufficient concern or care for potential consequences. We can become subtly embedded in other people's narratives and agendas without necessarily realising it and pass these along to others unknowingly. We can post messages that do not invite or create two-way conversations, limiting opportunities for ideas to be challenged, developed or evolved.

This reliance on the realm of virtual communication could result in us forgetting how to read body language, interpret tone, read between the silences, and be mindful of what we say and how we say it in the real world. We may risk being more careless with our words, becoming less graceful and less considerate because there is little immediate or no felt consequence when we are online. Added to this is that everything must happen so quickly in our 'fast-food-society'. Communicating and comprehending what another is saying now must be done in double-time, with a bunch of abbreviations that the older generations can struggle to keep up with and feel judged for not knowing or understanding. With fast-paced forms of communication, it can feel like there is no time to ask people to repeat or explain things more clearly, removing the chance

3. The Map is Not the Territory

to check-in and see what they intended to convey. This can leave people feeling unheard, unseen, and frustrated, angry at either being misunderstood or at not being given the chance to repair any hurt done from a misinterpretation of the intention. Possibly then leaving the energies of this anger and pain embedded in the relationship, leading to ongoing problems that remain unresolved due to ineffective communication or insufficient time devoted to communication grounded in kindness and accountability.

Our past relationship experiences can also negatively impact our current relationships with others. We can, albeit unknowingly, transfer pain caused by someone else into an expectation or fear that it will happen again, fears about who someone might turn into or what they may do, all of which cause doubts and pain, and prevent trust from being built. Whilst this is understandable, given that we have been hurt before and need to protect ourselves from being hurt again, if we are not aware this transfer could occur and do not actively manage it, we could risk alienating the other person, making them feel we do not see them for who they are, and by not taking the time to discuss and understand their actions fully, before assuming they are going to hurt us again. This can create extra tension or cause arguments.

The media and our culture can project strong ideals of what a relationship looks like, and how people should think, act, and feel. Reality shows can subtly develop our expectations and perceptions, often without us realising we are being conditioned by something that is designed to entertain and shock, not to form the basis for healthy lasting relationships. For example, there could be pressure on men and women to be all things to their partner, e.g., a lover, friend, caregiver, supporter, coach, counsellor, cook, cleaner, parent, and supplier of income. This is likely an impossible task. Then, when someone does not live up to all these expectations, problems may occur, the relationship can degrade, and we fight, just like the people on a television show that was designed to shock and pull in ratings, turning entertainment into a painful reality.

When our lives do not look like those on screen, which we have perhaps unconsciously idealised, we might assume either we are the problem or that our partner is without exploring the influences that could be directing our behaviour and communication. It might be more helpful to stop and ask ourselves: where do our relationship ideals and expectations come from? Is it possible the onscreen reality is not about helping us form healthy relationships, but about hooking people in to boost ratings? That having explosive arguments may be interesting to watch but painful to experience? That talking over someone and only seeing one side of the situation is entertaining to see from afar but limiting in real life? Remember, our subconscious is very powerful. It can take in more information and assimilate it in a single second than our conscious mind can. So, while we might think we are watching something just for fun, the agendas, beliefs, ideals, and behaviours we are being exposed to might also be sinking into that subconscious of ours. If we stop to think about the idealised images we see virtually, we may have the chance to reflect that they are often created and designed to generate ratings to sell more advertising, and not necessarily meant to guide us into healthy relationships.

In any kind of relationship, there can be an automatic transfer of our standards and expectations onto another person. This is one of those human behavioural things, not just a you thing. Unfortunately, the side effect of this transfer is that we can forget the other person has their own way of approaching things, and that it is OK that they do. Rarely do we voice our expectations to ourselves or reflect on the expectations we have of others. When we transfer these expectations into assumptions, and forget the other person has their own way of doing things, we can become unfairly frustrated, and create arguments based on differences that are both normal and natural. For example, one evening many years ago, I was running late for my volunteer radio show, rushing around the house trying to get everything done. In my mind, I was thinking how useless and unhelpful my husband was being. He was just sitting on the couch with the laptop, doing nothing to help me. Couldn't he see I was in a rush and needed help? Surely, he must have realized I needed him. It then occurred to me that he didn't know I was running late or that I was disorganised. He generally expected me to be OK, as I typically was. I assumed he knew that tonight I was not on top of anything. I was expecting him to come and help me without being asked. I stopped being mad at him in my head for not knowing what he could not know, and asked him for assistance, explaining I was late and in need of help. He then came to my aid instantly. How easily that could have blown up into an argument, with me going off at him for letting me down and not seeing I needed help, all because of unspoken assumptions and expectations. Taking my accountability for what I hadn't told him, and my kind way of conveying my struggle, and my ability to select one thought over another—choosing to ask, not criticise him—led to my husband being able to help in the way that I needed.

It is a very human trait to assume that everyone else is like us or gets us, without needing our input, hearing our perspective or being given directions. But as we know, assumptions are a poor currency and often fail us. If we don't tell people what our boundaries are or our needs are, they might not know. Perhaps we have had the experience of having a conversation in our mind, and then looping someone in half-way through, only to be flummoxed as to why they aren't drawing the same conclusions we are. By and large, we are not telepathic, and people are not necessarily like us in every way. While couples can start to align, especially after being together for a while, it does not mean we are the same. We might wear the same colour clothing without discussion or observation, we may finish one another's sentences or pre-empt a need some days. All of this can lead us to generalising thoughts that we are just like one another, all the time. So, it can then be quite the shock when we fall into an argument for having differing views or ways of doing things. We realise we are not completely like one another.

The map is then definitely not the territory. It may make us feel upset or angry that the other person is not who we assumed they were or has behaved unexpectedly. Assumptions and expectations belong to the realm of the ego. Remember, the ego likes to label, categorise and control things in order to feel good, safe, or in control, and this can limit growth or change. An ego-based attitude is typically not well received, and arguments may then follow. The topic of the argument is not so much the problem, it is the grab for power and control by the ego, the need for the ego to be right at all costs and feel good about itself consequently. As we know, a raging and needy ego is usually the result of someone whose self-esteem is low or from the sense that they are not safe. When our self-esteem is low, we may try to recoup our sense of self-worth through defensive and offensive tactics, so we can be right, the expert or authority, and to use our power to make sure we do not look foolish. If we feel unsafe, we might try to control everything and everyone around us, to feel like we are able to manage all the moving parts in ways that work for us. This may make us fight harder. If we are struggling with an inflated sense of self-importance, there could be no room for anyone else's views, and we may railroad over any differences of opinion. The communication is then not about collaboration and connection, just about who is right and who retains the power and control.

An individual with high self-esteem is open to hearing other viewpoints, does not depend on others to be like them to feel accepted, and openly embraces learning from differing opinions. They can release or soften expectations and see how assumptions are not useful. This generally makes for a more pleasant, constructive, and co-operative kind of communication. It allows us to be different from one another and makes agreeing unnecessary, and perhaps more joyful when it occurs. This does not mean we may not have heated debates or try to convince the other person, we just won't need them to agree with us or change, and we can continue to accept and respect one another regardless.

Through Books 1-3 of the Adaptable Sustainable Psychology collection, we have learnt about our own vulnerabilities, beliefs, and aspects of our personality that might cause us issues, and how we can have hidden assumptions and expectations that negatively can affect our life. This next part of the journey is how we take this information and integrate it into caring for and nurturing our relationships. The better we understand ourselves and what is driving us, the easier it is to navigate the journey with those whom we travel alongside. Thus, we may find we can cultivate more peaceful pathways that are imbued with kindness and accountability.

All of us, at some time, probably assume that everyone else is like us and expect other people to act in ways that we have never communicated about, assuming it's all very normal human behaviour. It is why we can be shocked and even angry when people do things outside of anything we might consider doing, whether it be surprise at someone's road rage or disappointment in them not replying to us in a timely, polite manner or something more serious such as conducting an affair and lying about it. There are numerous examples. Sometimes, these are neither good nor bad differences, just differences. Sometimes these differences can cause serious harm. **Being aware that difference exists allows you to manage it.** Thus, when we find ourselves being frustrated that someone isn't doing what we thought they would or is not as like us as we initially believed, it gives us the opportunity to ask: do they need to be?

If someone has a different view on politics this doesn't prevent us from learning from each other's opinions, and we can always agree to disagree, without it adversely affecting our relationship. If they choose to live their life in a way that is not entirely aligned with our philosophy, but treat us and others with respect, then maybe they don't need to be like us in every single way. If they have acted in a way that does not align with our value system by treating us or others disrespectfully or badly, then we may communicate with them that we are not OK with this or break off the relationship if they do not wish to change. If they have hurt us in a way that we would never

3. The Map is Not the Territory

hurt them, such as being physically violent, using derogative names, financially controlling or cheating on us, we may have to walk away from that relationship immediately.

Managing power dynamics in our relationships and using clear, careful and compassionate communication may help to build trust, co-operation and create harmony. By being comfortable with our own sense of power and control, knowing we can influence and affect many areas of our life, we can work with others, not against them. Being comfortable to be ourselves, maintaining our self-esteem and valuing who we are can help protect us from seeking these things out from others or our relationships in unhealthy ways. To help keep our relationships positive and strong we can consider using communication skills that foster and support two-way dialogues, where both parties are attending to one another, listening actively and considering what has happened to one another in the past that could affect either one of our behaviours now.

Knowing both what our assumptions and expectations are in a relationship, and what other people's are, is a part of how we may co-create meaningful connections. By learning to engage with and understand what our expectations and assumptions are, we can see more clearly when the map is not the territory, and instead of being lost, bewildered, angry, hurt, or confused as to why our relationships are not easier or working out, we can see what could be changed within ourselves to perhaps make a difference.

Knowing what our assumptions and expectations are of another person may help us manage the relationship with less reactivity, reduce unnecessary arguments, or avoid using manipulation tactics to try and force the person to be more like us. Only we can be responsible for our expectations and assumptions. Our expectations and assumptions belong entirely to us. They might not have been chosen by us in the first place; they may have been influenced by others, events or society. But choosing to hang onto them and not evolve them is down to us. We may be able to create a better a map for ourselves that can guide, inspire and support our relationships when it is based on accurate and honest self-awareness, embedded in **kindness** and fostering comfortable **accountability**.

Exercise: Assumptions and Expectations

Rather than navigating life with a map that isn't the territory—one built on unknown assumptions and unrecognised expectations that can harm you and your relationships—maybe step back and consider where both you and the other person are coming from.

Take time to think about the following questions and write down your answers. Perhaps talk them through with a professional therapist/counsellor or a friend afterwards.

Use them to help you understand yourself better so that you can spot what assumptions or expectations you have about both yourself and others that could lead to you not being OK that someone may be different from you, falling into poor communication patterns or seeking power and control in unhealthy and unhelpful ways.

1. What do you expect to get from your relationship, emotionally, physically, in terms of support, intimacy and affection wise, domestically and financially? What do you expect the other person to do to make this happen? Do you clearly communicate this to yourself or others?

2. Where do your ideas of relationships come from? Your parents? Society? Media? Previous experiences that you have learned from? How do you cope with or manage when people are different to what you expected or assumed?

3. How have you learned to communicate in relationships? What has influenced how you talk to someone, how actively you listen, how you react or respond and how to balance attention fairly? What types of communication do you think you have been exposed to previously?

4. How high or low is your self-esteem right now? How does this play out in relationships when there is no agreement? Do you feel you give in to the other person? Do you often insist on getting your way, on being right?

5. What fears do you have that stop you from being able to accept the other person as being different from you? Do you assume you might not be compatible if you are different? Do you fear being alone and, thus, must make the relationship work at all costs, comprising your values as a result? Do you believe you must always agree on everything to make a relationship last? Do you expect or fear violence or punishment, or being mocked for having a different opinion?

Next, using your answers and insights from the above questions, identify 3 previous relationships (e.g., romantic, family, friends or work-related) that have been negatively affected by any of the factors you just identified. Ask yourself the following:

3. The Map is Not the Territory

- Were yours or the other person's expectations and assumptions fair and reasonable in these situations? Can you see where they came from, past experiences, other people or the media? Were these informed, helpful and reliable sources?
- Did any of assumptions, expectations or fears keep you in unsafe relationships?
- What role did communication play in the breakdown of the relationship? Were there any assumptions and expectations that affected how the communication played out?
- How do you justify your expectations or the other person's, and is there something here that is unhealthy or unhelpful?
- Are you able to understand what issues or problems played out in previous relationships that led them to end?
- Are you able to learn from previous relationships, let the past go, and use the knowledge gained from the experiences to inform your other relationships to keep them improving and help you to grow?

If you find this exercise brings up difficult emotions, please pause and consider seeking support from a therapist or mental health professional.

Pause — Reflect — Landscape

1. **Pause** - Take a moment to sit with what you have just learned and consider it.

- Power can negatively affect relationships when someone is trying to control and direct what is happening without collaboration, kindness, and accountability being present.

- Online communication may reduce our real world communication skills, potentially leaving deficits in comprehension, patience and clarity, generating unhelpful assumptions or feeding unreasonable expectations, creating consequences that could leave people feeling unheard, misunderstood and at times frustrated.

- Past relationships and unhealed or unknown wounds can be transferred into a current relationship and may push the other person away or prevent trust from being built.

- The media can affect our expectations and assumptions of what relationships should look like, perhaps leading to potentially unfair demands and even explosive arguments, as opposed to calm and reasoned discussion, with an aim to find solutions, not generate drama.

3. The Map is Not the Territory

- Expectations and assumptions based around our perceived similarities can get in the way of good communication and could create arguments when agreement is not occurring as expected or assumed.

- Being mindful and tolerant that we are different people, with different outlooks and approaches, we may find it easier to communicate clearly and collaborate more effectively.

- The ego can push us to be right and can force our point of view across, possibly resorting to insults to protect us, maintain control and increase self-worth, especially if we feel insecure, unsafe or the ego is seeking a boost.

- Feeling comfortable to be ourselves, knowing we have personal agency in our lives and can therefore make choices may help reduce attempts at taking power from and trying to control others.

- Being conscious of maintaining and improving our communication skills may improve our relationships. By listening actively, paying attention to what we know about ourselves and the other person, we can be more compassionately aware and help support conversations in respectful, constructive and meaningful directions.

- It's normal to have expectations and assumptions, knowing what they are can help us in managing them positively and safely for ourselves and others.

2. **Reflect** - Answer the following questions:
   - Do you feel you move from a place of kindness and accountability in your relationships? Or are there things

- that can get in the way of you showing kindness to yourself and others? Is accountability uncomfortable for you? What can you do about this using the work covered in Books 1-3?

- How do you think your real world communication skills measure up? Do you actively listen and respond to others? Are you prepared to work through to find solutions, or do you resort to blocking someone or unfriending them without putting the work into the relationship and having the uncomfortable conversations?

- Do you think the media or your past has affected your idea of relationships in any way? Influenced any expectations or created any assumptions? Or inspired ways to communicate that are more about heightened reaction than being responsive?

3. **Landscape** - Step back from the details and see how this new information fits in with the bigger picture of your life. Consider your history, what is going on for you now, who and what is in your life, and the future you want for yourself.

- ✓ If you've had traumatic or bad experiences in relationships in the past, have you been able to fully understand the impacts that this has had upon your relationship skills? Are you vulnerable to others trying to hurt or control you? Or could you try to control them to keep yourself safer?

- ✓ Have there been times when you found it difficult to repair a relationship due to low self-esteem or thinking the other person wouldn't be interested in healing the relationship because you're not worth it?

3. The Map is Not the Territory

- ✓ Considering the relationships that you have experienced so far, and are currently in today, do you see any areas where your communication with others could be improved? Any areas that if you leave unattended might cause you problems in the future?
- ✓ When looking at past wounds, your expectations and assumptions and your communication skills, what do you manage well and where could you improve your coping skills to the benefit of both you and others?

4. The Relativity of Responsibility

In this section you will be learning about:

- → What types of responsibility we can practice.
- → How are relationships affected by different types of responsibility?
- → What are the risks of not managing responsibility well?
- → How can we assess our current level of responsibility?

You will need:

- ✓ To know we touch on trauma in this section, so be mindful that you are in a space where you feel OK for this subject to be discussed today.
- ✓ To reread your previous insights gained from other sections to help identify your patterns of behaviour.
- ✓ Time to reflect, with compassionate awareness, on how you conduct yourself in your relationships in relation to responsibility.
- ✓ A pen and paper to carry out a reflective, written exercise.
- ✓ To be open to discussing your reactions, feelings, and ideas, either with yourself or others.

4. The Relativity of Responsibility

"Over-responsibility can be a trauma response. You are not responsible for everyone and everything. Give yourself permission to lay down what doesn't belong to you."

Taylor Grismore

The word responsibility can conjure up a number of different emotions for us, some might be positive, some negative. One day during a discussion with my supervisor, Dr Bruce Wilson, we considered the possibility of a spectrum of responsibility on which we can move up and down throughout our lives and that this could change with different relationships, our experiences of responsibility relative to the time in our life, the people we are with, and our history that has shaped how comfortable we are with responsibility. Dr Wilson went on to describe four different types of responsibility that we might experience in his article *The Responsibility Continuum (February 2023)*: over responsibility, under responsibility, irresponsibility, and personal responsibility.

Whether we feel comfortable with the notion of responsibility or not, it is inevitably something that we encounter throughout our lives and we may use various types of responsibility at different times. This is why it might be helpful to think of responsibility as being on a spectrum—one that we can shift up and down depending on, what is going on in our lives, how we perceive our capacity in any one moment, how trauma may have impacted our perceptions and values around responsibility, and how others manage their responsibilities. How we approach and welcome responsibility into our lives can be influenced by our previous exposure to how others have managed responsibility in theirs. By making time to consider the different types of responsibility we can experience, and ascertaining which present us with opportunities and which pose risks, we can create strategies to optimise our responsibility levels, to minimise harm and maximise growth potential for better collective harmony. We start by looking more closely at the 4 types of responsibility Dr Wilson describes, and how they can positively and negatively affect us and our relationships.

The Overly-Responsible Person

This individual is often highly anxious, has issues saying no or setting healthy boundaries, has tendencies towards perfectionism, is likely to be a people pleaser, and could be a helicopter parent. There may be associations between those who experience childhood trauma and those who fall into being overly-responsible. Trauma can influence our sense of safety, and the overly-responsible individual may believe that by taking everything on that it could allow them to maintain control and feel safer. Trauma can impact our sense of personal agency the—belief that we can influence and affect our life through our choices and actions—and thus an individual could feel powerless to influence their own life and this leads to the attempt to take on as much as possible to generate a sense of being in control. Trauma can create a wish to protect others from harm, and this might lead to always putting others first, causing the individual to either neglect themselves or have insufficient resources left to tend to their own needs or rights. If a person has been made to feel the trauma was their fault, they may start to believe they are always at fault and responsible for everyone else, or believe that by taking all the responsibility they might not get in trouble and thus, remain safer.

The overly-responsible person puts their hand up for more tasks than they have time for and tends to take on the burden of other people's emotions, thinking they must continually change themselves to make others happy or take on the work of change on the behalf of others. They are usually self-critical and struggle to recognise when they are at capacity and can keep pushing until they are burnt out. Some of the consequences of being overly-responsible include the loss of the sense of self, fatigue, distress, and an increased potential for mistakes due to cognitive and emotional overload, stemming from doing too much and mental and physical health problems.

The Under-Responsible Person

At the other end of the spectrum is the under-responsible individual who leaves things to be sorted out by everyone else. They are task-avoidant and rarely volunteer their services. Everyone else is typically to blame for problems and, therefore, everyone else needs to change. This too can stem from trauma, where the feeling of being responsible is a trigger back to being abused and feeling that, somehow, they were responsible for this abuse. They might consciously know that they are not responsible for the abuse, but the feeling of responsibility becomes such an overwhelming trigger that they have to avoid responsibility as much as possible.

The under-responsible individual is unlikely going to put themselves out, nor change their behaviour. They typically do not accept that they have had any input into the problem, so why would they need to change? This behaviour disempowers the individual quite considerably, as they are not accepting responsibility and therefore, they have no control. This can lead them to feel demotivated, disinterested, unengaged, unhappy, possibly anxious, and depressed.

The Irresponsible Person

At the extreme end of the responsibility spectrum, we find the most dangerous individual, one who does not invest in any kind of responsible thinking at all. They do not care to consider consequences, nor do they safeguard others. These are the people who might drink and drive, gamble the family money away, commit crimes that harm others, and take actions that put either themselves or others at significant risk.

It could be construed as being irresponsible to be under-responsible and leave everything to everyone else. But you can also be irresponsible by being overly-responsible, as you could curtail and limit other people's opportunities to grow, evolve, and learn, either from their mistakes or from taking on new or different roles.

The Personally Responsible Person

This would be the middle of the spectrum. **The point of balance that allows us to embrace what is ours and not take on what belongs to others.** This means we can say no and put in boundaries when we know that we have taken on enough. We can allow others the opportunity to embrace their responsibilities, so that they can grow and evolve, and also know the joy and

4. The Relativity of Responsibility

satisfaction of succeeding. We fulfill our responsibilities appropriately and feel empowered for it. The personally responsible individual feels calm, grounded, secure, satisfied, and confident.

To be personally responsible takes strength and resilience to deal with whatever eventuates, including the not so nice or easy consequences that can come with responsibilities. There is no blame game in being personally responsible, not even of the self. A simple acknowledgement this belongs to me, therefore I can do something about it, is seen as being enough. Negatively judging and blaming the self or others is not seen as a good use of energy. Accessing this part of the spectrum means you may experience more interdependence, that harmonious place where you can be independent and simultaneously work effectively with others without dependence.

Someone who is comfortable being personally responsible is very likely to apportion responsibility differently in the various kinds of relationships that they have. Whilst there may be some commonalities, there could also be some stark differences, and this might also change as situations change. For example, you are personally responsible for ensuring your child remains safe. As they grow and become more independent, you adapt, and you encourage and support them to start learning how to be responsible for their own safety. Thus, when you are not around, you can trust your child, who is transitioning into being an adult, to be responsible for their own wellbeing.

Taking a step back, and pausing, to examine how we manage responsibility in our key relationships could help us develop a stronger structure to support our responsibility management, making sure that we are not being over-responsible, under-responsible, or irresponsible. You are responsible for how you manage responsibility.

The Responsibility Spectrum in Your Relationships

You might be beginning to see how a dangerous combination can be created when bringing together certain types of responsibility in relationships. An example of this would be combining an under-responsible individual and an overly-responsible individual. Both could wind up as irresponsible individuals, if they are not careful. The overly-responsible individual can take responsibility for everyone else's happiness and life. They tend to believe that this is their role (which could have come from a background of trauma) and that they do not deserve or cannot put themselves first. When coupled with the under-responsible individual, who has had everything done for them since childhood and believes that they are entitled to always come first, then problems may ensue. Neither party can grow out of their roles as they each validate each other's position. The overly-responsible keeps being overly-responsible and the under-responsible is happy to remain in their usual status quo. As neither person can grow, neither can the relationship. Thus, it is likely the relationship will end as the over-responsible party eventually becomes burnt out and too depleted to continue.

In this scenario, the uneven exchange of energies between the over-responsible and the under-responsible cannot be sustained. The under-responsible individual has not learnt anything from growing through their uncomfortable emotions because they never had to experience any. This could make the over-responsible person irresponsible by always taking the responsibility and not creating a space for the other to grow. The under-responsible person becomes so dependent on others that they start to behave irresponsibly when someone else is not continually stepping in for them. This also may mean

4. The Relativity of Responsibility

the under-responsible person might end up being unhappy in other areas of their life if they have developed the idea that they cannot take action or do not have to take action in any way.

Parenting children well is an enormous challenge, and one that can be fraught with doubts and fears, especially in our modern world, where parents have to be more vigilant in supporting their children with making safe and appropriate choices. Managing responsibility as a parent is a complex task. Too little and the child is at risk of neglect; too much and the child won't have the space to learn from their mistakes and develop resilience. It's an unenviable task. The overly-responsible parent could create an under-responsible child. They make their child dependent on others to solve their issues, and they do not learn that there are consequences with the choices we make. When it comes to using drugs and alcohol, this could have devastating outcomes. What happens when the parents are not available to fix their child's problems, or they simply cannot fix them? Could drugs or alcohol then fix the pain instead of the parents? Or does the child/adult think that their parents can fix any issue so there is no need for responsible drug-taking? What happens when the under-responsible child is old enough to have a partner who might also be under-responsible, and the partner wants to blame them for everything and treat them badly? How do they navigate and progress in their job when they cannot take responsibility to improve themselves for a promotion or to maintain their career? This is not to say that drug addiction, being in a domestic violent relationship or having career issues is due just to parenting styles, there are many other factors that can influence and lead to these outcomes occurring, how responsibility plays out in childhood may or may not be relevant.

Seeing your child suffer any kind of pain or emotional discomfort is immensely difficult, and the natural inclination is to want to protect your child from having any adverse experience. The risk facing the overly-responsible parent that tries to protect their child from all uncomfortable emotions is that their child may not end up equipped with the skills of adaptation and resilience that can help them to navigate to live independently and support their mental health. This overprotection from learning to be with uncomfortable emotions or manage stress could become a disservice to the child, as they may struggle later as an adult from not having learned from a younger age how to self-regulate or problem-solve for themselves. The costs of creating that perfect childhood might potentially lead to a much harder and unhappier adulthood.

Being able to allow our child to experience uncomfortable emotions, and to be responsible for their own behaviour by carefully exposing them to the consequences of their choices, can be very hard. Whilst it is understandable to want to protect our child, to give them everything we can and help them to be happy, balancing this desire with guiding them into being a personally responsible adult may be a more helpful focus for parenting. We can still be a positive support and guide and encourage our child whilst they process their feelings. We are still with them in any difficult space as a backstop offering them a sense of security and being held from afar, but the child learns to self-regulate, increases their confidence, and learns to find their own solutions that could work for them in difficult circumstances, all alongside our continuing parental support and suggestions in the background. The overuse of the concept of positive parenting, where a child is not given a no or there are no clear boundaries, may, unfortunately, have removed too much of this balance. We now have generations of young people moving into adulthood who struggle to cope with their uncomfortable emotions, rely too much on others to fix their life, and who can end up in unhealthy relationships that are about being entitled, not giving to the other person, or working equally as a team.

Similar unhealthy patterns can be seen to play out with professional relationships, where the under-responsible can default to the over-responsible, creating a constant imbalance. The irresponsible employee or manager who comes from being under-responsible can shirk their duties, leaving it to their team to pick up the slack or even gaslight others into taking on their work or mistakes. The irresponsible person, who is over-responsible, can burn themselves out by taking on everything and not allowing others to be a part of the process and share the load, preventing co-workers from learning and developing their skill set.

In friendships, the under-responsible individual can let the over-responsible friend initiate all the contact, make all the plans and provide them with constant positive feedback or support. Friendships cannot be sustained under such strain and one-way streets. Irresponsible friends can be flaky with their energy and commitment, often making excuses and putting all the responsibility on the other friend to make events happen and to be understanding and patient when they change their minds. Again, such friendships cannot be sustained as the effort put into any relationship requires a balanced input on both sides. Both parties are better off when giving an equal amount of energy and care.

A responsibility-growth paradigm creates an environment where people are encouraged into making choices, supported in accepting the consequences, and given the opportunity of learning each step of the way. **If you can own it, you can grow from it.** This learning then can be shared amongst others to build health and wealth across the community. All too often, we see governments blaming previous administrations rather than accepting that they have chosen to step in and lead the way. This waste of time and energy in blaming their predecessors could be diverted into finding viable solutions to move forward. When those who lead us struggle with responsibility, it is understandable that we as individuals also struggle with responsibility.

It all comes down to finding a way to manage collective responsibility versus individual responsibility. Under-responsibility leads to no growth. Over-responsibility leads to resentment and burnout. Irresponsibility affects everyone. **Find peace in personal responsibility**; it may support your sense of control and choice and enable you to cultivate positive relationships with one another.

4. The Relativity of Responsibility

Exercise: Where are you on the Responsibility Spectrum?

To work out how you are managing your responsibility level, have a look at your behaviour, the types of words you use, and the actions you take to identify if you are ever being overly-responsible, under-responsible, or irresponsible.

Use the table below as a template and see if any of the statements trigger a reaction, or make you think of things you might say in relation to responsibility in different circumstances. Add your own insights, experiences, and assess your responsibility level as you go. Types of relationships to consider your responsibility level in include parent/child, intimate, friendship, work, government/social, and community.

Once you can clearly recognise your own patterns with responsibility, you can use your capacity for mindfulness to be present and see the perception, underlying belief or value that could benefit from being adjusted or changed. You can then use the exercises from Books 1-3 to achieve this change.

Once the belief is reframed to a positive, self-affirming, self-supportive and community-minded perspective, you can adjust your responsibility setting into the personal responsibility zone. Find that sweet spot, where you work out what you can take on and what belongs to others. Build confidence in others when required, rather than doing it for them. Share responsibility positively.

The Adaptable Sustainable Psychology Collection: Book 4

Statement or behaviour	Under-Responsible	Overly-Responsible	Irresponsible	Underlying fear/Possible Belief
"Yeah, but you do this..."				I'm not good enough. I can't cope with blame.
"Everything goes wrong for me."				I have no control in my life. I can't make choices that make a difference.
"I cannot say no to my child."				If I'm not the perfect parent, I'm not good enough. My child must have the perfect childhood.
"It's not my job."				I doubt my ability. I am afraid to try.
"I always need to apologise for other people's feelings."				I'm a bad person; it's always my fault. I'm not worthy.
"The government/my partner/my family should be doing this."				I can't make a difference. I am entitled to more. It's not my job. I might make a mistake.

4. The Relativity of Responsibility

If you find this exercise brings up difficult emotions, please pause and consider seeking support from a therapist or mental health professional.

Pause — Reflect — Landscape

1. **Pause** - Take a moment to sit with what you have just learned and consider it.

- How we interact with and feel about responsibility may be influenced by our experiences and how others have managed responsibility throughout our lives.

- There are four types of responsible behaviour we can access: overly-responsible, under-responsible, irresponsible and personally responsible.

- The overly-responsible takes on too much and can burn out. The under-responsible does too little and subsequently can never take control of their life. Irresponsible people put themselves and others at risk.

- Those who are personally responsible balance what is theirs and what belongs to other people with kindness and care, adapting to situations to adjust the sharing of responsibility appropriately.

- Finding the balance of teaching children responsibility safely, with support and space to learn from mistakes and discover how to find comfort when uncomfortable, may help to encourage personal responsibility in adulthood.

4. The Relativity of Responsibility

- Creating a space for responsibility and growth can lead to people making informed choices, supporting one another with the consequences, and learning about what works and what doesn't.
- Personal responsibility may help to foster peace, support a sense of control, and enable positive relationships.

2. **Reflect** - Answer the following questions:

- How have you felt when reading the section on responsibility? Did you have any strong reactions? Were there parts that you did not agree with? Why do you think that is?
- How do you think you manage responsibility in your life currently? What types of responsibility have you engaged with across your life—one or two, or all of them?

3. **Landscape** - Step back from the details and see how this new information fits in with the bigger picture of your life. Consider your history, what is going on for you now, who and what is in your life, and the future you want for yourself.

- ✓ Looking back across your life, what has influenced your ability to be comfortable with responsibility? Has it been a positive or negative influence? Is it one that might benefit from reframing or working on if it isn't allowing you to move into healthy personal responsibility?
- ✓ Are there any blocks to you learning how to be comfortable with responsibility? Do these include insecurity, poor self-esteem, trauma, or fear? What could help you overcome or manage these blocks to create fair and equitable responsibility in your relationships?

5. The Power of Self-Trust

In this section you will be learning about:

→ How can self-trust reduce our justifying behaviours and improve our relationships through positive accountability?

→ What can self-forgiveness and the act of releasing do to help soften justification and increase our self-trust?

→ How self-compassion lights the way and lessens the load of this hard work.

You will need:

✓ To be aware that this section discusses forgiveness, which may feel triggering or difficult. We are not suggesting forgiveness for perpetrators of violent crimes unless this is something you personally choose. Your individual choice is always respected.

✓ To be mindful that we talk about trauma and to check you are ready to engage with this topic today. Be gentle with yourself as you read and know it's completely okay to come back to it later—or not read it at all.

✓ A pen and paper, to carry out a reflective written exercise.

✓ To be open to discussing your reactions, feelings, and ideas, either with yourself or others.

5. The Power of Self-Trust

"Nothing in the universe can stop you from letting go and starting over."

Guy Finley

They say the success of a con artist comes from their ability to believe in their own con. The moment they doubt their lies, others can too. It is one thing to fool someone into believing something, while it is quite another to convince yourself. Self-trust is a commodity that can be in scarce supply, and yet it can offer us a way to be comfortable with ourselves, and with this confidence in trusting ourselves comes an opportunity for us to sit comfortably with accountability, which can subsequently improve our relationships with others. When we struggle to accept responsibility and be accountable, this could stem from a lack of self-trust and may lead us into justifying ourselves. Justification is something everyone does at some point. It can be healthy and fair at times, but sometimes we can justify ourselves in an unhealthy manner that does not support personal and collective change. Things become someone else's responsibility or are attributed to circumstances beyond our control, and then no growth can occur.

To be personally responsible requires self-trust and the active management of self-judgment. These skills may help us to accept responsibility by helping us to feel comfortable with who we are and believe in our capacity to cope and change. If, when faced with being responsible, we land in a space of negative self-judgment because we feel insecure, we can start to feel uncomfortable. We don't want to feel uncomfortable, and thus we can default automatically to justifying ourselves, as this can seem to be the quickest and easiest way to escape these feelings. In the process of justifying ourselves, we may relinquish responsibility and not be appropriately accountable. This is another one of those human behavioural things, not necessarily a you thing, so don't waste time or energy beating yourself up for something that can be common to how we all operate from time to time. Everyone justifies at some point or another; there is no value to you expending energy feeling bad for using this behaviour. It is far better to invest that energy into understanding why we are justifying and ascertaining if it is appropriate and fair, and assess how it might be impacting our relationships. It may be beneficial to check that we are not avoiding personal responsibility because we don't feel good enough or wish to sidestep changing, and then assess if that avoidance could cause damage to our relationships or at the other end of the spectrum, if taking on too much responsibility on could damage us.

It is important to acknowledge how potentially damaging trauma can be to self-trust and how much of a role it can play in defensive justification. If we fear being punished for making mistakes, as we have been in the past, we may go to great lengths to avoid being accountable. This can occur unconsciously and automatically as a protective mechanism to keep us safe from further harm, without any conscious intention. Surviving trauma is also fatiguing and can significantly damage our self-worth. This can set us up to believe that we

5. The Power of Self-Trust

do not have the personal resources left to take on anything extra, including responsibility. If we have identified that we are not feeling safe taking responsibility or are too overwhelmed to take on being accountable, we can check to see if there is a correlation between these feelings and any previous trauma. This may be something we can work on and change.

If trauma has impacted our ability to trust ourselves to assess situations and feel safe enough to take on appropriate responsibility, we may find learning how to build self-trust supportive, and this may include seeking some help from a professional therapist. We can start by focusing on developing a strong internal narrative that supports and encourages us to see the elements in our life that we have done well, the things we have achieved, no matter how big or small. It could be going for a walk or keeping your home tidy, completing a course of study, it could be styling your hair nicely or picking up a piece of litter from the street. Look to the moments you did good things, the times you got yourself through, those times you were right, or did a job well, and gradually this may show you that you are more than the trauma has led you to believe or see, and you can use these experiences to build confidence and trust in yourself.

Justifying and self-trust have a deep relationship with one another, and if we have low self-trust and then feel mistrusted by someone else, the urge to justify ourselves can be intense and overdone to the point that we end up generating the very mistrust we were attempting to avoid. Our justification fails to be the explanation or demonstration of how trustworthy we are that we intended, and instead becomes our undoing. We all value being trusted; it represents someone's faith or value in who we are and what we do. It makes us feel good, accepted, and it improves our confidence. Therefore, when trust is questioned, we can feel the opposite of all this; we may feel worthless, disregarded, and unsure of ourselves.

High achievers tend to be particularly susceptible to being hurt or offended by mistrust. Take, for example, a doctor who feels frustrated by a patient who uses 'Dr Google,' leading to an outburst. Now, using our energy to assess this reaction, rather than judging it, is the doctor justified in feeling frustrated? We might consider that the doctor attended university for 7+ years, and undertakes extensive additional learning every year to maintain their licence, and may fear that unverified information on the internet could cause harm to their patient. But, one could counter that the patient is simply looking for more information to help themselves, and this has nothing to do with how they see their doctor's competencies.

Is the patient responsible for making the doctor feel good about their knowledge, or is the doctor there to help the patient? Looking at things from the patient's point of view, the doctor's frustrated outburst was perhaps not the best way to communicate their concern. Understanding that someone might want to research their health and focusing on how helpful it is probably makes for a better response. Rather than assuming the patient is distrusting them, which makes them feel angry, the doctor could ask why they googled and what they learned so it can be discussed. The patient, taking on board the doctor's perspective, could recognise that the doctor has high levels of responsibility and does not want to see their patient at risk, as it could have serious consequences for them both. The patient, therefore, reflects that next time they do some independent research, they will tell the doctor they wanted to be more proactive in their treatment, and ask the doctor to help them understand what they have learned so they can work together towards a good solution for their care.

How we respond to other people's behaviours, and their reactions, is where it counts. Justification might, at times close the door to two-way communication and can erode people's trust in themselves, as well as each other. Holding compassion on both sides may assist in unlocking this quandary. An empathetic and respectful approach from both sides of the situation can aid the relationship and steer it back towards mutual trust and co-operation. When we approach one another with an openness to hear the other's point of view, understand their fears, and recognise their needs, we gain valuable insights into each other. Information allows more accurate assessments to be made and educated decisions can then follow. By moving from a space of self-awareness and awareness of the other person, our relationships can feel safer. Thus, we improve the trust in both ourselves and the relationship. It's a win-win.

Justification tends to follow hot on the heels of previous mistakes we are struggling to either be accountable for or let go of. The more we rely on justifying our actions, the more we could risk second-guessing ourselves in all areas of life and losing our self-trust completely. There are likely many components to justifying our mistakes. One could be the need to reassure ourselves we are not a terrible person, another may be a need to prove to others we are not a terrible person. Both of these needs can be driven out of the ego and low self-esteem. There is nothing wrong with explaining our actions to others but doing so from a position of inner trust, where we believe and know that we are a kind and accountable person, may support the creation of better outcomes. If we have already accepted that, ultimately, we can trust ourselves and that we can own and correct errors, others may see and feel this as well. Even if they do not, their reaction or mistrust does not have to be as upsetting because we are not dependent on them for approval or acceptance. When we feel secure enough, we can accept that, at times, we all can make unintended mistakes. If we have owned what we can be personally responsible for, and trust we can move forward and adapt, then there is less need for justification, and **positive ownership** and a **willingness to grow** can become the focus.

Trusting Yourself to Forgive or Release

Self-trust and self-forgiveness have an intimate relationship, and one may at times be dependent on the other. All relationships require forgiveness at some point, whether it is our relationship with ourselves that requires our self-forgiveness or a relationship with another person. Forgiveness can be a very hard thing to think about and may be a somewhat controversial subject to discuss. Many are averse to the concept, believing it can convey approval for bad behaviour or let people off the hook too easily. There may be some acts that cannot be forgiven.

Forcing forgiveness is not helpful. It is something a person chooses to arrive at. When it comes to violent crime, it is completely understandable why someone does not forgive another person, and we are not promoting that they need to. In such circumstances, releasing or letting go of the event or person could replace forgiveness in freeing us of the uncomfortable burden of holding on. We do not need to forgive the person, but releasing what has happened and acknowledging this is now over may help us with moving forward with our life, and this could be more beneficial than remaining in a past we cannot change. If this person cared so little about us or failed to respect our human rights, then our opinion of them, our anger, our hatred, and our unforgiveness is unlikely to make any difference to them. Hanging on to the event and ruminating over it could keep us trapped in the space of that horrible moment.

Working towards releasing painful events might help to free us from the hold they may have on our emotions and psyche. Like forgiveness, releasing does not automatically make everything OK. It may take many, many years to release the energy and damage that an event has caused. The benefits of letting go of the past are that we can then be free to be more present, making it the best we possibly can for ourselves, and perhaps feeling safer about our future by being aware that we can take our knowledge with us.

When it comes to the more minor hurts that we receive, it is fair to say that we can all make errors from time to time. When we cannot forgive ourselves or we cannot release something or let go, then we may automatically lean into justification. When we cannot forgive ourselves or others, we can lean into resentment. Neither resentment nor justification is a healthy space to occupy for any length of time. Forgiveness is defined as ceasing to blame and letting go of resentment. So, if we continue to blame another or ourselves and hold onto resentment, we could remain in the ugly moment. By holding on, we can make what has been and gone an experience in the present. Thus, all the negative emotions associated with the incident may be constantly re-ignited and re-experienced. People make mistakes and bad choices. We have the ability to choose to accept this and choose to release it and let it go.

Sadly, no amount of hanging onto to the bad things that have happened because of us, or been done to us, is going to change the fact that they have happened. We can choose to leave those who hurt us and have nothing further to do with them. We can stop replaying the tapes of the event in our minds. But healing may also be supported by showing ourselves compassion and understanding for it happening. Self-forgiveness can help us in being able to trust ourselves again.

It may not be an easy or simple process to forgive ourselves. There may be significant blocks that we have to overcome. If, for example, we were raised in an environment where we felt responsible for our parents or caregivers' emotional wellbeing or believed that we were somehow responsible for their arguments. Or we believed their drug or alcohol misuse meant we weren't worth being present for and looking after. Or perhaps, someone made us believe their abusive behaviour was somehow our fault or there was simply no escape from our abuser. Then self-forgiveness might feel like an impossible task after years of convincing ourselves everything bad that happens is our fault. This is where our work from Books 1-3 can help us challenge and change unhelpful beliefs that stop us from forgiving ourselves. We may even benefit from forgiving ourselves for thinking we need to forgive ourselves for the things we took on as a child that weren't ours to bear. You may choose to seek help from a professional therapist if this resonates with you and they can help guide you through this difficult process of self-forgiveness to help you regain self-trust and, consequently, build trust with others.

Navigating forgiveness can be tough and there may have been times in our lives we have acted with good intent on the information available at the time, with no thought or desire to cause ourselves or anyone else harm yet, still made an error in judgment. Often, we make the best decision we can in the circumstances we are in with what we know. We cannot know what we don't know. Beating ourselves up and justifying why we stayed in a bad relationship, for example, is not likely to help us move forward into a better one with either ourselves or anyone else.

Depending on the situation, learning how to forgive or release ourselves for the things that have had negative consequences for us or others can stem from accepting we made an unhelpful choice, as this can help us bypass wasting resources like our time and energy on excessive justification that doesn't change or resolve the situation. Justifying can help us understand that we did not intend harm, but if it does not lead to acceptance and change, and then we may remain stuck in a cycle of behaviour that has the potential to repeat itself endlessly, going nowhere helpful. Forgiveness or releasing can break this pattern and allow us to use our energy to grow and change. This might be a better use of our resources, and it still allows us to understand why something happened, which means that we can then address our behaviour honestly and find ways to improve our decision-making and, thus, avoid hurting others or ourselves again. It may support how we heal relationships and move on from a place of **kindness and compassion.** These are **the bedrock of all healthy relationships**, including the one you have with yourself.

If we find forgiveness is not something that is easy or natural for us but would still like to experience it, we could adopt a different view of forgiveness. We might focus on forgiving ourselves or the other person, but perhaps not the behaviour. In this way, perhaps we can feel that our forgiveness is saying we thought the behaviour was not OK, but that the person doing the behaviour, be it ourselves or another, made an error and can be forgiven. If we use this kind of forgiveness, it does not mean we have to remain in any kind of relationship with the person who hurt us. We may put in clear or legal boundaries, but we may then find it easier to let go of the person or the moment and process our heavy emotions. In this way, forgiveness brings us to a broader perspective, where the blame for this action that happened in a moment has been recognised but the moment is released, and new opportunities for change can be explored from here on in. Please remember we are not talking about this in reference to severe and enduring trauma or violence. To forgive or let go of deeply traumatic events is much more complicated and takes a long time, seeking professional support in this area may help you on this potentially difficult path.

Compassion is the sympathetic consciousness we can hold for another person's distress, alongside a desire to alleviate it. Self-compassion is when we direct that conscious awareness to our own suffering with a desire to help ourselves. Maybe you can introduce some self-compassion to ease into forgiveness or the releasing of events. Compassion brings warmth and understanding. It allows for mistakes to have happened, facilitates the capacity to let go of things that were not our fault and supports the ability to recognise factors that can be altered to create safer choices in the future. The act of releasing or forgiveness might help us to let go of the pain around what has happened and assist us in putting our energies into creating different outcomes. The moment we were hurt is in the past, and this cannot be changed. But we are here and now. This means that we and others can still change. No one is saying this is easy or simple, nor that learning gets ignored in this process. If anything, learning may have the better chance to occur when we forgive or release. Repetitive and endless justification can be a block to growth and may not give us the personal agency to see change through. When you seek to dwell with inner peace, **self-trust, self-forgiveness,** and **letting go** could help you on your way there.

Exercise: Releasing and Forgiveness

This is not necessarily an easy exercise, and one you may have to repeat many times throughout your life. If it feels too much to do now, maybe come back to it another time or discuss it with a professional therapist or a trusted friend.

It is offered here as an option, but please know this exercise can be freely passed over if you're not ready for it. You know your limits, so check-in with yourself and do not push yourself to an unhealthy point. It is OK not to use this exercise at this time.

It might be easier to begin forgiving the smaller things, not changing the toilet roll over perhaps or forgetting a task or date and then you can work up to the bigger ones if it feels safe to do so.

- Start by making a list of all the people you feel you could offer forgiveness to from your past and present.
- Make sure to put yourself at the top of the list.
- If you want to work on releasing events rather than forgiving people, make a list of those events that hurt or haunt you, or cause you to feel anger or resentment.
- Now, hold a mental image of yourself or call to mind the feeling that a person or situation has created, and

find your sense of compassion, that place of recognising you are in distress and wanting to help yourself. Notice if you can feel it anywhere in your body, and if you can focus in on that area.

- Then breathe slowly and deeply, reassuring yourself you are there for you, you are safe in this present moment and acknowledge that you are ready to forgive or release.

- See yourself cut all ties to the person, situation, feelings, and any unhelpful memories, and let the whole thing go, like a balloon rising with the wind up into the sky.

- It may be extremely hard with some people or situations, you may have to keep returning and repeating the exercise, if you feel you can, until such time that you feel peace or calmness in the place of the hurt.

- Keep going, if you can, until you feel a greater distance between you and the event(s) and when there is a sense of self-compassion, acceptance, and serenity around you.

- Take time to do this exercise regularly to help manage the burden of resentment and pain. They are not productive states, and they can create unhappiness for you and block growth.

Pause — Reflect — Landscape

1. **Pause** - Take a moment to sit with what you have just learned and consider it.

- Trusting ourselves can help support us in being responsible and taking accountability positively with others, and this can lead to growth and change together.

- We can find that harmony and shared accountability in our relationships are aided when all parties can start from a place of self-trust, compassion and kindness, rather than fear, insecurity and defensiveness.

- Trauma can lead us into being overly apologetic or heighten justification to protect ourselves from further harm. Becoming aware of this, without negative judgment, and finding ways to heal and release the damage of past hurts may help us to create space to build self-trust and assess when we take responsibility and when it is to be shared with others.

- Judging ourselves negatively and not feeling good enough can lead us to overly justify our actions without always acknowledging our role in events, even if it is only small. This may block the building of trust in relationships and affect being able to work together as a team.

5. The Power of Self-Trust

- Feeling that we are not trusted by others when we have low self-worth can lead to over justification and create more suspicion, barriers to connection and generate mistrust. Potentially, making us feel worse about ourselves.

- Forgiveness is a difficult area to move into and is best led by what you feel safe and comfortable with. If forgiveness feels uncomfortable or is not right for us, releasing what has hurt us, by assigning it to the past and recognising we are now able to move towards a space of healing may bring us comfort and an opportunity to be more present.

- Forgiveness is about no longer blaming or holding onto resentment. Whether it is forgiving or releasing yourself, an event or a person, it may help us avoid staying in a past moment that we can no longer change.

- By stepping into self-forgiveness, we can continue to build and generate self-trust.

- Accepting that we can make mistakes, with no intention to do harm, can reduce justifying behaviour, open the door for forgiveness or releasing, and assist us in changing from a place of kindness and compassion.

- Self-compassion is directing conscious awareness to our own suffering with a desire to help ourselves. Compassion for others recognises their distress, with the desire to alleviate it. In compassion we find kindness for one another and ourselves.

- Inner peace may be supported by self-trust, self-forgiveness and being able to let go.

2. **Reflect** - Answer the following questions:

- Have you found any of the ideas here very challenging? How much do you feel you currently trust yourself? Do you wish to seek any extra help or professional support relating to the issues discussed here?

- Are you someone who finds it easy to forgive themselves? Or are you overly harsh, demanding and unforgiving towards your mistakes or errors in judgment? Would you be open to changing this? Could any of the exercises from the ASP collection help you with this?

3. **Landscape** - Step back from the details and see how this new information fits in with the bigger picture of your life. Consider your history, what is going on for you now, who and what is in your life, and the future you want for yourself.

- ✓ Have you held onto any responsibilities that are not yours that you might be better off releasing? Do they impact your current relationships in any way?

- ✓ Do you have a pattern of apologising too much or justifying too much? Can you see how these behaviours may have adversely affected previous relationships or how they could impact current ones?

- ✓ Can you see times in your life when your self-trust was low? What problems did this create for you? What have you done to build trust in yourself or what could you do to feel confident in your ability to take responsibility, forgive yourself, and if appropriate others? Do you feel having more accountability and kindness could help your relationships?

6. Power and Relationships

In this section you will be learning about:

→ How does power show up in our relationships, and how does our sense of individual control affect it?

→ What options are there to manage and defuse oppositional relationships?

→ How could circular relationships support and encourage all parties equally?

→ How can choosing interdependence over independence help us learn, grow, and connect?

You will need:

✓ The previous insights you gained from other sections to help identify your patterns of behaviour.

✓ A small group or one other person to complete the exercise provided.

✓ A pen and paper to make any notes on insights gained.

✓ To be open to discussing your reactions, feelings, and ideas, either with yourself or others.

6. Power and Relationships

"Diversity: the art of thinking independently together."
Malcolm Forbes

There is a limited amount of power in any relationship and there may be times when both parties are seeking to control that power. With a world that is becoming more regulated and controlled, this can unconsciously affect people and their use of power in their personal relationships. There may be those who are willing to take whatever power they can, without regard for how it might affect the other person. By recognising the power dynamics that someone is trying to play, we can work out how to better position ourselves to defuse or manage the situation, as opposed to being swept up in someone else's power game.

Identifying where you are sitting in terms of your own personal power is the first step.

- Are you feeling controlled by others or systems today?
- Have you been controlled in the past in unhealthy ways?
- Have you been feeling powerless lately and, thereby, possibly at risk of buying into the fight to grab some for yourself?

Next, you identify where the other person is coming from. Are they just like you, trying to find their way in the world, but perhaps attempting to obtain some power in a negative fashion through you, either unconsciously or consciously? Do they have a troubled history where others have tried to control them in manipulative or negative ways? When trying to ascertain if someone is trying to control the relationship, it may help to consider whether people have been subjected to being excessively controlled in their past (by parents, bosses, partners, or abusers). Could they be rebelling, not against you, but against their past? Or have they only had unhealthy power dynamics modelled to them in previous relationships? By exploring the dynamic before judging it, you can make more informed choices and maybe avoid inflaming the situation. Compassion and careful communication generally work better than an offensive or defensive approach. In psychodiverse terms, **power can be better managed by gaining information and using it constructively and compassionately**.

People can seek power by becoming oppositional. This can happen for any number of reasons and the more you understand about the dynamics being played out, the more mindfully you can choose a course of action to positively approach the other person. So, hopefully, instead of butting heads, you can work together to find a suitable solution to the issue. People can seek power to feed their sense of independence or to show they are capable of acting alone. Teenagers are typically a good example of this, particularly when it comes to being oppositional. The combination of swirling hormones, along with the fact that they are told what to do at home, in school, and by society makes a heady cocktail for potential angst. If we can hold a place of compassion, and maintain an understanding perspective, we may have a better chance to calm the situation and find safe solutions. It may mean some sacrifices are made by both parties, and it won't necessarily be without emotional discomfort, but a positive outcome is more likely when at least one person can hold a clear, calm space that is less about power and more focused on safety and guidance.

Oppositional teenagers are not the only complex relationship where power can underlie the issues. We can deal with oppositional relationships at work, with friends, and with our intimate partners, and it can become difficult if we allow our emotional reactions to lead the way. Once our emotions are telling the story, they can cloud the issue and may move us into the ego space if not well managed. Remember, the ego, amongst other things, likes to be right, to win, or to protect its identity. If we are aware of why we feel unhappy, and can see our part that needs to change, as well as the other party's, then we are more likely to present this in a non-activating and neutral way and improve chances for a successful collaboration.

You may recall from previous discussions how easy it can be for our emotions to start telling us a story, and it may not always have a happy ending. This story can take us on a journey where we encounter more memories, ideas and emotions and, thus, we can easily become overwhelmed. Think back to what you learned about yourself in terms of whether you are typically a reactionary individual or whether you respond to situations. A response, as you may recall, is considered. The pause button is usually pressed, and we take time to assess ourselves and those who are around us, and any factors that might be affecting us and them. When we react, it can be primal or even atavistic (an unconscious habit such as behaving aggressively or territorially). It is usually protective because we feel someone is assaulting, attacking, or hurting us and we wish to defend ourselves immediately to avert the perceived threat or minimise future harm. Working with positive emotional management techniques, and using tools like breathing exercises, can help you hit that pause button, manage your emotional reactions, and work through them quickly to make them into a co-operative response.

People can also confuse arguments with aggression. Arguments are often misunderstood and seen as being negative. Yet, they can, at times, be a positive force for change and a chance to get to know someone better. However, when arguments become aggressive, we move into different territory. Aggression is a reactive energy to a perceived threat. Aggressive energy is palpable. It can be felt even when something is unspoken, and aggression tends to feed on negativity. Therefore, if one person is being aggressive, and the other reacts aggressively, the aggression can start to grow, creating mounting tension and heightened anger. Logic may then seem to have left the discussion.

In arguments, when an agreement cannot be found, we might feel powerless and end up thinking we are being doubted or feel insulted and belittled. This can come from how the other person's communication is managed or how their behaviour is making us feel, but the root of these feelings could also be connected to our insecurity. In this case, this is something we can immediately change by reviewing where our feelings are emanating from, and making sure our past or our self-doubt is not interfering unhelpfully in our present. There may also be times when the other person is deliberately trying to make us feel this way, to have control of the conversation and the outcome. In this case, further assessment may provide ideas on how to handle the situation safely, and if we might require more time to

6. Power and Relationships

consider strategies for either addressing the situation or exiting it if necessary.

There is a profound difference between someone who has unintentionally caused you to feel distress, and someone who is deliberately trying to inflame your emotions and antagonise you. To ascertain if someone is being deliberately cruel, you can look to the intention as your starting place. Most people do not plan or intend to hurt another. But if someone wishes to manipulate you, they may use your emotions and previous experiences against you to do this. In a healthy relationship space, the agenda is about mutual understanding, success, and happiness, not making the other person feel bad about themselves or their past.

When we feel powerless in relationships, working out if our feelings are being prompted through our insular ego (who wants to be right or transfer past experiences that are not helpful) or our expansive awareness (who is looking at what we know of ourselves, the other person and the present situation from a broader perspective), might make it easier to take that step back to review the situation. The ego can link us back to previous experiences that have had a bad outcome and assume the situation is the same and activate the defences. In contrast, our awareness can recognise similarities to past problems and works in the present to assess if there are any current risks before taking any action. Using the awareness perspective provides an opportunity to learn and evolve through hearing someone's differing views, and it can lead us to ultimately and respectfully agree to disagree. But the ego could cause us to become fearful and disproportionately defensive or disrespectful and controlling of others in order to feel safe or be right, and we may end up making the original issue bigger than it needs to be.

Identifying strategies to help you manage and defuse oppositional, and possibly aggressive, communications is another good skill to have in that psychodiverse arsenal of yours. The more information you both can share, and the more carefully you can both communicate, the greater the chance that mutually beneficial discussions can be achieved. When we are not careful, our opinions can be reflected through our ego's wounds. These may not come from the heart of what we wish to communicate, but can be an expression of the fear, hurt, or anger we might be feeling. This may lead to unfair accusations or misplaced anger directed at someone not threatening us or causing actual harm, but they are creating a trigger for us that is valid and may benefit from our care and attention, and hopefully with the co-operation of the other person we can find a calm and safe way to be present and address the situation.

Checking-in with your expectations, and the other person's, is another way to see if anything is amiss power wise and could help us navigate out of any escalating nastiness. As you may recall, when an expectation is met or not met, we can have an emotional reaction. If we can micro-manage this reaction by quickly asking if the expectation was realistic or fair, then we gain another piece of information to work with. If either one of us is having an emotional reaction to an unfair expectation, we can see if we are able to move into a space of compassion. From there we can offer validation, firstly to ourselves that we understand our own emotions, and then we can appreciate the other person's emotional reaction, and better understand the expectations held by both of us. Then instead of emotions telling the story we are, and instead of the ego grasping for power mutual understanding becomes the focus.

This might save either one of us from attacking the other or defending ourselves when we do not really need to.

If the discussion becomes about defending ourselves, rather than understanding the other person, we can cycle back to where we were, arguing, with the danger of aggression entering. When we deny that the other person might feel a certain way, and we cannot accept their feelings as being valid, the other person could feel devalued and made to feel wrong for having a normal human emotion. We do not have to fully relate to or understand their emotions, but acknowledging that they are real for them can go a long way. If we can communicate this congruently and compassionately, it may then allow us to address the responsibility we both hold regarding the situation. This allows for the opportunity to gain yet more information about the other person and ourselves. Information can give us power to make better choices. **Power may be best used in choosing actions that benefit us all**, not in controlling one another.

In communication, responsibility is always shared. Whether we are the sender or the receiver, we hold an equal level of accountability for the communication. If we take accountability for our part in communication, there is a greater chance the other person may also. Working equally in this space, we can define better ways of communicating together that respect one another and support each other into managing our own emotions, not passing them back and forth to one another. This takes the power away from one side of the relationship and distributes it evenly between us. When the power struggle is removed and we share the responsibility for how we communicate and can be accountable for how we send and receive communication, we have the chance to work together in common purpose. We both want to find a solution without damaging the other along the way.

Circular relationships are about working together to achieve the best results for you both. Relationships could be better seen as being circular rather than being part of a chain of command. A circular relationship is a relationship that exists without the overlay of power. Power becomes unnecessary in circular relationships because you are always looking out for the best for each other, therefore working together to achieve the best for you both. Who is right and who is wrong becomes unnecessary as conversations are based around what is best for you both individually and for you both collectively.

When we choose independence over a relationship, we could become a danger to the relationship. Others can become objects to be manipulated or managed for our own betterment, happiness or satisfaction, and we can convince ourselves it is for the greater good of all. Power and knowledge are then merely the justification used to make others conform without regard for individual circumstances, without respect and without kindness. By assuming you are right and know best, you could be blinded from seeing the other—their potential, their humanness—and it could cause division in the relationship. When working together, in relation to one another, being flexible and releasing a need for power, it may mean something much more effective and meaningful can be created. If we truly learn to regard one another's concerns as our own, there is no need for hierarchy as our goals are the same. We work together to find solutions that are not about punishment or judgment.

The concept of power in relationships is like water to a fish, so prevalent that it goes unseen and unquestioned. We have grown so used to making power a fundamental part of our relationships that we now may fail to recognise its negative effects and the detrimental role it could play in damaging us and our relationships. Whether in couples, families, or workplaces, creating and fostering a deeper appreciation for how another person thinks and sees life can help you find more common ground or compassion, and it is from here you can build a life or project together.

In a world busy with everyone looking at their devices, we may be forgetting to look at one another. Creating spaces and opportunities where we reveal who we are in the real world could be less available and we may have to work more consciously on carving them out. When we take time to connect outside of oppositional arguments or disagreements, it might mean we have a stronger foundation, built upon knowledge of one another and the moments where we have shown each other kindness and gratitude. This can then form a backdrop for difficult moments and instead of leaping into power grabbing mode for our own defence and survival, we are much more likely to see where we can learn from the other person and support one another into creating a brighter future. **Power is then shared and used for mutual benefit**. Spending time together is about having fun, creating memories, and building a strong framework for collaboration that can handle future problems that could divide us. Being in circular relationships may mean we generate clearer insights, hold more respect for ourselves and one another, work in common purpose and form deeper bonds from the kindness shared.

Exercise: The Compliments and Gratitude Game

This simple and brief exercise works with either two people or with a small group, e.g., workmates, friends, or your family.

It is a great way to regularly start hearing and learning about one another, as well as taking an opportunity to give to and receive compliments from each other. It is about gaining information, giving time and compassion, and not gaining or misusing power.

Each person takes a turn speaking and answering the following:

1. Name one good thing that happened today.
2. Name one thing you are grateful for today.
3. Name one hard thing that happened today. How did you cope or not cope with it?
4. Pay one compliment to the person on your left.

This process helps you learn to give and receive compliments. Practice listening and communication skills. Focus on positive attributes of your day, yourself, and other people. Identify anything that might have been a struggle and check that you have addressed it. Support others in navigating them through their tough spots by witnessing them and sharing the journey, talking through their process or, if appropriate, offering guidance and help.

It can also start some interesting conversations and is especially fun with young children. It is quite amazing to see what they come up with.

Pause — Reflect — Landscape

1. **Pause** - Take a moment to sit with what you have just learned and consider it.

- There is a limited amount of power in relationships and people can vie for that power to take control and increase their self-worth.

- Working out what the power dynamics are and why people are behaving in a certain way, and where their need for power is coming from can help safeguard us and the other people involved.

- Understanding where we stand within our own power and how much control we feel we have in the present moment can be another helpful step in managing power dynamics healthily.

- It can be helpful to assess where other people are sitting in terms of their personal power, checking if they have a trauma history of being manipulated and controlled or have had recent experiences of feeling powerless, observing if this is an ongoing pattern where they often try to take control and dictate situations or whether this is an unusual occurrence.

6. Power and Relationships

- Power can be positively managed by collecting and using information to understand one another more deeply, kindly and compassionately.

- We can seek power by being oppositional, defensive or by attacking one another. Keeping calm, looking for mutually beneficial solutions and helping ourselves and the other person feel validated and heard can help manage the situation.

- Recognising when our or others' self-worth is low or we are feeling insecure can help us identify a vulnerability that might lead one of us to seek power to feel better, feel right or be safe. Being supportive and encouraging towards ourselves and others may ameliorate this.

- Arguments can be positive and help us to learn about each other but when they become accusatory or aggressive, we may be better off to pause, reassess our situation and if we cannot create calmness and kindness together, walk away.

- If people use our vulnerabilities against us this could be dangerous, potentially toxic to our inner landscape and we may have to stay away from those who do this.

- Our negative past experiences can affect our ability to communicate and remain present and careful in our relationships. Managing our and others' expectations can help with clarity and creating more compassion and kindness.

- Circular relationships are about regarding everyone's needs as being equally important as our own and can help remove power dynamics.

- Creating and fostering appreciation, compassion, and understanding for how other people think, their experiences and how they see life could open up opportunities to build trust together and develop intimacy and care as a team.

2. **Reflect** - Answer the following questions:
    - How do you manage power in a relationship? Are you aware when you are seeking power or control in a relationship? Or when others are trying to have that power and control over you?
    - How do you feel about the ways in which you manage power and control in your relationships?
    - Where is your self-worth sitting currently? Have you noticed when you feel insecure or triggered, you seek out more control, become more defensive or try to take power from others?

3. **Landscape** - Step back from the details and see how this new information fits in with the bigger picture of your life. Consider your history, what is going on for you now, who and what is in your life, and the future you want for yourself.

- Do you recognise any areas of your life where you have experienced a circular relationship, where everyone looks out for each other's needs and sees them as important as their own?
- Is there anything that you feel would be worth addressing within yourself to help create and maintain more circular relationships?

6. Power and Relationships

- Have you developed a way to assess situations in real-time and been able to understand where you are coming from in terms of power and control and where the other person might be? Could some reflective practice of looking back on old relationships to see what was playing out help you achieve this? Could you work towards being able to reflexively assess what is happening in the moment when you and another person may not agree or have different needs/perspectives?

7. Communion or Communication?

In this section you will be learning about:

→ What is the difference between communing and communication?

→ Why is reacting unhelpful, and how does responding create a window for communing?

→ What are common communication problems, and how do they impact our relationships?

→ Why does intention matter so much when communicating?

You will need:

✓ Any previous insights gained from other sections to help identify your patterns of behaviour.

✓ Time to practice breathing and focusing exercises to be able to witness your own communication style and identify if there are issues to work on.

✓ People to practice role playing with (feel free to groan here—these aren't everyone's idea of fun).

✓ A pen and paper to make any notes on insights gained.

✓ To be open to discussing your reactions, feelings, and ideas, either with yourself or others.

7. Communion or Communication?

If writers wrote as carelessly as some people talk, then adhasdh asdglaseuyt[bn[pasdlgkhasdfasdf"
Lemony Snicket

Communication is defined as the process by which one can transfer information from one place, person, or group to another. Communion is the sharing or exchanging of intimate thoughts and feelings, especially on a mental or spiritual level. We hear a lot about communication, be it in the workplace, in intimate relationships, or between family members. We hear much less about when we might get more out of consciously moving to communing, rather than just communicating. When separating out the two concepts, communication seems to be the more practical vehicle. In our modern, technology-supported world, communication has multiple platforms that may mean we often bypass direct face-to-face contact. Messaging systems, texts, emails, AI, social media, all can limit the opportunity for communion, and can also open a gateway to misunderstanding and highly sensitised reactivity that can be shared without filters.

By now, you may have come to understand that a reaction is merely a replay of a previous behaviour. In other words, you are just mimicking what you have done before, 're-acting' it.

It is one of the reasons why people feel like they keep having the same conversation over and over again, because they are reacting just like they have in the past. When we communicate without engaging our consciousness, without mindfulness or connecting to our integrity, the communication might be limited and could go awry.

The brain is a bit like a big filing system at times. It can identify previous similar situations and cue us to similar, previously used or observed behaviours or actions. This means that if we communicate by relying solely on the brain, without engaging our mind, our integrity, or our awareness, there is a chance that we won't be considering the uniqueness of the current situation or considering the other person or ourselves sufficiently. In this space of reactionary communication, we may overlay past references that are irrelevant and could trigger yet more uncomfortable emotions in ourselves or the other person. Those emotions may start telling a story, one that might not be true and could be based on fear. By creating communion, we make space for each party to potentially walk away feeling uplifted, supported, and hopeful. We elicit responses from one another, not 're-acted' scenes that have not produced positive outcomes previously. We can respond through engagement, rather than the need to share our story, chime in, or be the funniest, brightest, or best. Communion is what communication is all about, and it involves our mind, awareness and our integrity. It is truly tuning in to yourself and each other in the moment. This is much harder to do on a texting service or messaging platform, even with emojis.

There are as many ways for our communication to go wrong as there are books on how to communicate. We may not be able to commune with one another when we rush with our words and force our meaning onto others. We may not be able to commune when we do not pause to take in the other person in their entirety, listening to more than just their words. There is always the chance that we might misunderstand the meaning or use the same words, just in different ways. When we are not fully present but recalling some past behaviour, or hearing words that hurt us, or thinking about what we are cooking for dinner, then we may not be able to commune. We may not be able to commune when there is no mindfulness about our own reactions and the feelings that have surfaced, and we do not consider what emotions we are experiencing—or why—before we speak. If we are busy being involved in planning out our next sentence or rehearsing a retort in our head, then we may not be really listening to the other person. My mother repeatedly advised me to "engage brain before mouth". There are many times I wish I had heeded such advice better.

Things that can make you go hmm...

The following table sets out some common communication problems and the consequences that can follow these issues.

Communication problem	Resulting emotions and behaviours
Red-flag listening – inconsistently paying attention, dropping in and out of focus.	The other person does not feel heard, so they shut down. They may feel devalued and have any low self-worth issues triggered. This can cease communication and communion because it seems futile to continue when no one is listening.
Hostile language – swearing, name-calling, and personalizing comments made to the detriment of the other person.	Typically, when people feel attacked, they mirror and/or increase the intensity, thus escalating the situation. This can lead to aggressive behaviour or violence, or cause the other person to shut down or walk away.
Maintaining silence without explanation (e.g., you might need time) or ghosting.	This can be seen as being a passive-aggressive tactic and can create frustration and cause tension to mount. It can be used to make another person suffer and question themselves as to why the silence, which can feel manipulative and leaves no room for communion.
Deliberately excluding the other person as if they are not there (such as in a group) or talking over someone.	This behaviour leads people to feel ignored and invisible. If self-esteem is already low, this can worsen it. From this behaviour, resentment may build, and bitterness can lead to divisions that might not permit communion to occur. It can be divisive and cause pain.
Blaming and making accusations.	When there is no room for self-accountability it creates a roadblock in the middle of the communion. Parties can become antagonistic and seek retribution in the form of their own accusations and blame. Thus, no one is getting around the roadblock. You are all stuck.

7. Communion or Communication?

Take a moment to sit with the following questions relating to the table, and see what answers you come up with:

- Being honest and aware, do you use any of these tactics or have any habits like these?
- Do you unconsciously lapse into any of them when you are reminded of past hurts or trauma?
- Are any of them your go-to-tactic when you feel attacked?
- Could you look to change some of these into more constructive communication tools to be able to facilitate and support opportunities for communing?
- Would it help to practice more real-life conversations, texting less and talking more?

One of the best ways to improve our communication skills and to start communing more is to simply practice. Checking-in with our own intention when we are communicating helps us become more attentive to how the other person is either reacting or responding to what we are trying to say. Focus more on **how people are receiving you,** rather than just perceiving you. Typically, a non-positive reaction to our communication is going to come from a misunderstanding of our intention or their own intention is getting in the way of hearing ours.

If someone reacts adversely, or contrary to how you hoped, would finding a new approach to be more gentle, positive, or kind be helpful? How would it feel to ask and explore the following:

- What is this person's history?
- What do you know about them and how might that affect how they are hearing what you are trying to say?

- What do you know about their style of communication, and would mirroring this be helpful in the situation?
- Can you directly explain what your intention is and acknowledge what their intention is, seeking clarification?

If in answering these questions in your communication situation you identify some possible issues, go back over them and work together with the other person to improve how you deliver your message and how they receive it.

People tend to let you know when you are doing well with your communication style by mirroring you, and by keeping the focus on connecting safely—not on being clever, right, rude, or perfect. How you approach misunderstandings, resolve difficulties, and front up about mistakes in communication can all be supportive ways to **build trust and increase harmony in relationships**, and the more you get out there and communicate, the better you may become at sharing your intent so that it can be received with respect and clarity by all parties.

7. Communion or Communication?

Exercise: Role Plays... Oh Yes!

Some people may feel embarrassed about role playing. But this activity can be rich with insights and a great way to spot unhelpful habits or to practice new techniques. If you can, make a group of three. You each take a turn in observing whilst the other two act out the role play. After each role play, everyone shares their feelings, thoughts, and observations.

If you cannot find anyone to role play with, you could bring this up as a discussion with someone and ask their opinion on the scenario described. Ask them what they might do in such a situation. There is no right or wrong way to do these exercises. Use them to show you how communication might spiral, might be saved, or can become dangerous.

1. Listening to Calm - Counsellor and Client

The counsellor's role is to get the client to open up and feel as calm as possible. They must actively listen, watch out for their own red-flag listening and when they are not paying full attention, looking at body language, listening to the tone of voice, assessing how much eye contact occurs and when, listening out for what the client might not be saying, and repeating back what they are hearing respectfully to the client for affirmation and confirmation. Use silence positively for reflection. Remain non-judgmental and congruent.

The client is very distrustful, on edge, and almost accusatory, as if the counsellor is to blame for their problems. The counsellor must reassure the client they can express themselves and work to break down the barriers to help the client feel calm and safe. The counsellor cannot respond in kind to the client at any time and must not mirror any hostility, even when provoked.

2. Creating Positive Understanding - Arguer and Pacifier

The arguer returns after horrific traffic and an awful day at the office. Now they are upset that dinner is not ready. The pacifier tries to calm them, explaining the reasons the dinner is not ready due to their own challenges in the day, while remaining compassionate and empathetic.

The arguer tries to provoke the pacifier and take out their negative energy on them. The pacifier cannot react to the blame and must be clear that the arguer is being unfair and calmly explain they won't accept the hostility or bad mood the arguer is putting on them. Then try to get the arguer to help them with dinner, so together they can go more quickly and help them both work through their bad day as a team, supporting one another.

3. Constructive Criticism - Boss and Employee

The boss must compassionately tell an employee their work is not as good as it used to be. The boss must try to find out why and help the employee find ways to improve.

The employee starts feeling very offended and gets agitated and distressed. The boss must remain calm and keep trying to help the employee make this a positive conversation and not get pulled into the employee's negative energy or blame game.

7. Communion or Communication?

Pause — Reflect — Landscape

1. **Pause** - Take a moment to sit with what you have just learned and consider it.

- Communication is the transfer of information and communion is the spiritual, emotional, and mental connection where we share ideas, thoughts and feelings.

- Communication can go awry when we are not fully present and aware, when we are distracted or preoccupied, or so busy planning our reply we are not fully listening. Missing helpful cues from body language, eye contact, and tone of voice can also lead to misunderstandings and miscommunications occurring.

- Communication problems include red-flag listening, where we are dropping in and out of listening or zoning in and out of the moment.

- Using negative speech including swearing and name-calling, hurting others by using what you know about them against them to cause them to be upset is likely to shut down any hope of useful and meaningful connection.

- Using silence, without communicating and acknowledging openly the need for space and respite to process and respond, could be cruel and seen as a passive-aggressive tactic designed to hurt the other person.

- If we get trapped in the past or fearful for the future, we are less present and could miss useful and relevant components of the communication or misunderstand someone's intentions.

- If we are not paying attention to our reactions and our feelings, and understand where they have come from, we may risk being more reactive and less responsive and we may not be able to address the presenting issues.

- Ignoring or cutting people off, or talking over them, can make them feel devalued and prevent them from being an active participant in the process of communication.

- We might find it useful to be mindful of how we are working with our accountability, and observing if we start moving into a blaming paradigm, especially if the focus is on delivering defence rather than creating co-operation.

- Practicing our communication, becoming mindful of who we are and who we are communicating with and adjusting our ways of engaging with one another may help us create more effective communication and develop deeper communion.

2. **Reflect** - Answer the following questions:

   - How evolved do you think your communication skills are? Could they do with an upgrade and being honed a bit more?

7. Communion or Communication?

- In which areas do you think your communication could benefit from improvement?
- Have you ever had the experience of communing with someone? What was this like for you? Can you recall what helped it to happen?

3. **Landscape** - Step back from the details and see how this new information fits in with the bigger picture of your life. Consider your history, what is going on for you now, who and what is in your life, and the future you want for yourself.

- ✓ When reviewing past relationships can you identify communication problems that occurred? Can you see how you fixed them or how you could have fixed them?
- ✓ What would you like to change about your communication style? Are there any significant blocks, unhelpful beliefs or fears that might get in the way of you achieving these changes?
- ✓ Are there any issues with self-doubt or low self-worth that could prevent you from being vulnerable and open enough to create a communion with someone instead of simply sharing information?

8. Self-Acceptance: Your Ally for Kinder Relationships.

In this section you will be learning about:

- → What can self-acceptance do to help support healthier relationships?
- → How can expectations hinder self-acceptance, and how does gratitude feed self-acceptance and help it grow?
- → Where does humility play a role in self-acceptance—for both ourselves and others?
- → How can working with intention improve your relationships?

You will need:

- ✓ The insights gained from this book and your notes.
- ✓ A pen and paper and time to carry out a written exercise.
- ✓ To be open to discussing your reactions, feelings, and ideas, either with yourself or others.

8. Self-Acceptance: Your Ally for Kinder Relationships.

"When you are content to be simply yourself and don't compare or compete, everyone will respect you."

Lao Tzu, Tao Te Ching

It has long been a human endeavour to seek nirvana, discover paradise, or create a utopian existence—one sustained by healthy, co-operative relationships. Perhaps the path to such a life begins with accepting who we are—as well as the present, whatever it looks or feels like—and choosing to trust our inner resources to make the best of each circumstance until change for the better is required or possible. This could be more achievable when we have evolved to adapt and endure hard times without self-judgement or any sense of "not-enoughness," use sustainable coping methods, place the wellbeing of others on an equal footing with our own, seek out those who support our strengths, and do whatever it takes to identify—and remove—what gets in the way of living by these ideals. To find our way to being a kind, compassionate, and accountable person who treats themselves and others well, we might explore our capacity for self-acceptance and see how sitting in this space can serve our inner journey toward peace and cultivate more harmonious relationships.

Self-acceptance is a foundational component that can help

build healthy, enjoyable, and resilient relationships. When we don't accept ourselves, others may find it harder to accept us—and we may also struggle to extend that same grace to them. A major roadblock to self-acceptance can be found in our expectations. Expectations rarely foster acceptance; they can pull us out of the present and into the ego's need to quantify, label, and box things into black-and-white categories—good/bad, right/wrong, success/failure—leaving little room for nuance. So, when our expectations aren't met, or when people or life "fall short," self-acceptance often becomes much harder. We may struggle to feel good or adjust to what's happening, and even the hope of self-acceptance can fade. If we're finding it hard to accept ourselves or others, we can start by examining how useful our expectations really are and looking to cultivate these three qualities that may help support our journey to self-acceptance: gratitude, humility, and kind intentions.

Gratitude:

An attitude of gratitude is more likely to serve us well than focusing on what we don't have or adopting a "poor me" mindset. Focusing on what we're grateful for—whether it's the world we live in, our lifestyle, the decisions we've made, the people in our life, or the skills we have, the small things or the bigger achievements—may help us feel more positive, peaceful, and accepting. Practicing gratitude can also support self-acceptance and the acceptance of others. But gratitude can be a very hard road to go down when we are dealing with great adversity or pain. Someone telling us to count our blessings can seem patronising or annoying, especially if their words are delivered in a way that feels condescending or oblivious to our current suffering. And whilst it might be good advice we agree with, following it is another matter.

Gratitude can be powerful medicine—calming and soothing our souls—and choosing to lean into it may be the kindest thing we can do in difficult times. It is not necessarily an instant fix, but when we start to think from a place of gratitude, our ability to accept ourselves and our situation can start to change—and when our perception changes, so can our emotional experience. This means we might shift from feeling dark and heavy to feeling that touch lighter and more peaceful, not overnight, but maybe that road just got a little bit easier to go down.

Humility:

There has been an increase in the use of the term narcissist—or "narc," as it's sometimes abbreviated in Australia—to describe people who lack humility or empathy, seem not to consider others, have an excessive need for attention and admiration, and display an inflated sense of self-importance. Narcissism exists on a personality spectrum, and while many of us may show some traits at times, some people operate with these tendencies more prominently. Humility and narcissism are uneasy companions and rarely appear together. When someone is absorbed primarily in their own abilities, knowledge, or contributions, they may miss rich opportunities for connection that others bring. Although people with pronounced narcissistic traits may appear to possess strong self-acceptance, the reality is often the opposite: they may feel deeply insecure and rely on continual external validation to feel good.

High narcissism isn't a trait most people enjoy being around or working with, so it can be a lonely way to live.

Relationships may be short-lived because others burn out trying to meet the narcissist's constant need for attention. When we focus on being "better than" others—or avoid owning mistakes for fear of judgment—we leave little room for humility, including about our genuine strengths. The result is a loss of perspective and increased insularity, with less appreciation for diversity.

When our emotional and mental bandwidth narrows because we over-believe in our own brilliance, it becomes harder to accept outcomes that don't confirm that belief. If we can't acknowledge our limitations, mistakes, or failures—because the ego is fixated on how good it must feel—it will naturally defend itself by blaming others or circumstances. A large ego is rarely an asset for building lasting, healthy relationships; always needing to be the best, right, or perfect leaves no room for humility when things don't go as hoped. Humility helps us believe in ourselves while accepting our strengths without parading them to diminish others. It allows us to meet our mistakes with compassion, work well within our limitations, and let self-acceptance grow—so we can collaborate with respect, kindness, and accountability.

Kind Intentions:

As we have discussed previously, one way to avoid friction or de-escalate arguments, and manage any unfair or overly demanding expectations, is to be clear about what we intend with our communication and the outcome we hope for, while expressing both with respectful care towards the other party. Accessing our capacity for self-acceptance may be helped when most of our inner needs are being met by ourselves, thus we

8. Self-Acceptance: Your Ally for Kinder Relationships.

may feel less reliant on others to fulfil them. This in turn, may reduce unhelpful expectations or limit assumptions and free up our inner resources to flow with people and situations. As this mental and emotional clutter clears, identifying—and, when needed, adjusting—our intentions become easier. Feeling freer to accept outcomes different from what we expected allows us to refine our intention toward making the best of what arises, while also giving us more space and energy to help others move toward their best outcomes.

Having done our inner work, to be better able to support ourselves with kindness and sit more comfortably with accountability, we may find this helps us to be open and honest about our behaviour, our needs, and our vulnerabilities, and thus, being clearer about our intentions becomes more natural. Mindful behaviour can help us to see what our mind is trying to achieve by saying things in certain ways, at certain times, and with a certain kind of tone. This might mean at times we recognise undesirable intentions in ourselves. An example of this might be when our tone is set to wound or hurt the other person when we are feeling hurt. Or we seek attention by trying to turn their mind against someone or getting them to feel sorry for us by disclosing information in a particular way. Our intentions might not always be terribly honourable. But don't drop into negative judgment just yet. Remember, that does not necessarily facilitate growth. We can all come at things from a less than wholesome intention, but when we deny this, we can do nothing about it. But if we can own our intention (privately in our own head is fine; this is not anything we necessarily have to publicly declare), we can change course, if it is not one that serves us and those around us.

Working with intention can help in creating clear

communication and may facilitate a pathway to communing. We can get to intention using mindfulness, and by having a broad, compassionate scope of understanding about ourselves, knowing what makes us feel down, what uplifts us, what might trigger trauma, or what our ego can seek out in terms of validation and recognition from others. This map of ourselves can guide our mindful capacity to drop in on ourselves when we are communicating, not only to ascertain what intention is driving us, be it conscious or unconscious, but also to identify the other person's intention. Once we understand our intention through the prism of self-acceptance, we can adjust it to focus on kindness and accountability—for ourselves and the other party.

Comprehending each other's intentions from a space of self-acceptance can lead to healthier communication, and when meeting in a space of mutual understanding of one another's intentions with kindness and compassion, communing may begin. Instead of focusing on the feelings that are getting triggered, we might see what needs to be understood and addressed. When our feelings are not telling the story, we may detach momentarily from being hurt, angry, or feeling belittled. Whilst these feelings may be real, detaching from them, even if only briefly, can create a window through which we can glimpse and know why they are there, and this allows us an opportunity to discuss them without lapsing into blame and disagreement. Thus, promoting acceptance and understanding of each other and encouraging a willingness to not injure each other in a damaging manner, and this may allow communing to occur and intimacy to grow.

There may be times when we are hurting that we wish that someone else felt the same pain we do. Most of the time, we can control this impulse. At other times, we may not. Those high on the narcissism scale are more likely to say hurtful things to make themselves feel better and soothe any deeply held insecurity, as the need to feel better can override concerns over any possible harm that could, consequentially, affect anyone else. There may be occasions when we are distracted, tired, stressed, in pain, or hungry when we say things carelessly and cause another person to feel upset. Understanding intention when we communicate is how we can bypass arguments to reach a mutual place of respect and understanding or work out when stepping away from someone whose intention is to use us to feel better about themselves might be a better option.

In general, most people do not wake up with a list of things to say or do, to either hurt or annoy another person. When the grounded person who is content to be themselves meets the careless communicator, they can calmly address poorly worded or ill-considered communication. The accountable, kind, comfortable person is not seeking validation from another person. Thus, they have free resources to identify where the poor communication has originated from or at least ask why these words have been said in such a way. The calm and clear communicator can look for intent and, if they cannot see it, they can ask what was intended by that statement or behaviour. Whilst this can still create challenging conversations, it may ease the heavy energy or reduce aggression that might otherwise creep in when neither party is looking for the intent behind the words. There may be value in learning to accept yourself to help you protect yourself.

Identifying intention may help us to evade manipulation. It may be wise to avoid people who might try to drain our energy by attempting to pull us into their circus and dance with their monkeys. Intention lets us work out when we are being offered a deal that is favourable to us both, or just to the other party. Identifying our own intention in any communication means that we can stop ourselves from saying things that might not serve us or that could create more problems for us. Remember, accessing an understanding of our and other people's intentions is the mechanism through which healthy communication and the chance to commune can occur. Communing may uplift and nourish us, and therefore, may further enhance self-acceptance.

Working out our intentions and others' can be a higher-level communication skill. It requires us to learn how to hit the pause button more readily, rather than rushing into communication. As my mother would advise, "engage brain before mouth". Our compulsion to be heard, to provide our side, to feel enough, to feel safe and in control, or just retort, may get in the way of that button being pressed. Building a strong sense of self-acceptance can help us when we are looking for patience, it can help us in releasing the need to be heard or seen by others and knowing how to feel good enough and validate ourselves through self-kindness. All of which can support us into being that clear, kind and considered communicator who looks for intention before reaction. Training ourselves to self-accept, avoid harsh and unhelpful self-judgment, and practice compassion with ourselves and others helps us to **self-forget to connect.** If you seek to develop a more easeful and joyful way of living, sustained by healthy relationships, you may find that both acceptance of yourself and others is an important part of this.

Exercise: The Piece of Paper

1. Take a piece of paper. Make it into a tight ball, and then try to unfold it, and flatten it back out, smoothing it down as much as you can.
2. Now, apologise to the piece of paper for screwing it up.
3. Unfortunately, nothing changes. The paper remains messed up; it can never revert to what it was before you screwed it up.
4. Both you and others can feel like this too. If you communicate to others or yourself carelessly and say hurtful things, then your words may leave a mark, and your later apology may do little to wash them away.
5. Rather than wait to apologise, take time to learn to communicate kindly in the first place.
6. Be aware that your words can have a lasting impact on people, yourself and your relationships. It is usually much more than you think.

Pause—Reflect—Landscape

1. **Pause** - Take a moment to sit with what you have just learned and consider it.

- When we can accept ourselves and others, we can increase our chances to live peacefully and grow together.

- What we expect of ourselves, and others, can get in the way of self-acceptance, these expectations can lead to judgment, criticism, and feeling unfulfilled. All of this may leave no room for self-acceptance.

- Gratitude can be a gateway to self-acceptance by allowing the positives to outshine any negatives, uplifting us into a space of appreciation and recognition.

- Being grateful can be very challenging and at times feel impossible when we are in pain or suffering, but the benefits make it a worthwhile pursuit.

- Having humility is about being confident and comfortable in ourselves without a need to express or share it in a way that could make others feel less. It is inner acknowledgement of our qualities and successes, without the requirement of others knowing or validating us.

8. Self-Acceptance: Your Ally for Kinder Relationships.

- Intention can help to soften expectations and develop kinder communication that may support all parties in finding ways to make the best of situations.
- Pathways to intention include mindfulness, having a broad compassionate knowledge about ourselves, being aware of what activates and upsets us, and how our ego may sometimes seek out validation or recognition from others.
- Instead of sitting in the emotions that are being triggered, using mindful awareness we can step back to assess where they are coming from and using our self-knowledge we can help ourselves to remain calm, express what is going on for us and ask the other person to work with us, not against us, thus helping to support and nurture kind intentions and self-acceptance.
- Remaining accountable, clear and calm can help us spot both our intentions and others', and avoid being manipulated or drained, and create healthy communication to work towards meeting our and another's needs.
- When we have a secure basis of self-acceptance this may support our work with any reactions, helping us to manage them and can create a window into what our intention is and assess where the other person is coming from. From here, co-operation and compassion can extend out of kindness, rather than criticism. And this may lead us to grow together and find fulfilment in our relationships.

2. **Reflect** - Answer the following questions:
   - How comfortable do you feel being yourself? Do you accept all your positive qualities, and sometimes challenging qualities?
   - Is gratitude something that you find easy to do or can it be difficult due to the experiences that you have had in life?
   - Do you naturally lean towards humility, or do you tend to move towards seeking approval and validation from others by extolling your successes and virtues?

3. **Landscape** - Step back from the details and see how this new information fits in with the bigger picture of your life. Consider your history, what is going on for you now, who and what is in your life, and the future you want for yourself.
   - ✓ How well do you think you have expressed your intentions to others over the course of your relationship history? Could this be an area that might benefit from some improvement?
   - ✓ Do you feel when communicating with someone else that you are coming from a place of deep self-acceptance or are you moving from doubt, insecurity, or perhaps somewhere in between?
   - ✓ What can help you evolve into a deeper level of self-acceptance, gain the ability to clarify your intentions and easily assess and discover others' intentions and motivations to create more harmonious and fulfilling relationships?

9. For a Reason, for a Season, for Life.

In this section you will be learning about:

→ Why embrace grief and loss gently, with kindness and courage?

→ How can identity be tied to our relationships in ways we do not realise?

→ How the spectrum of grief may move you between pain and peace.

You will need:

✓ Kindness towards yourself, and awareness that this section discusses grief, which could be triggering. Remember to check in; this might not be what you need right now.

✓ A pen and paper to make notes.

✓ To be open to discussing your reactions, feelings, and ideas, either with yourself or others.

9. For a Reason, for a Season, for Life.

Only people who are capable of loving strongly can also suffer great sorrow, but this same necessity of loving serves to counteract their grief and heals them."

Leo Tolstoy

One of my friend's often refers to an old saying when a friendship or relationship comes to an end. There are friends for a reason, who come into your life for a particular purpose. There are friends for a season, who come around for an appropriate time in your life. And there are friends for life, relationships that you maintain and keep through all your years. Losing relationships and people we love hurts. The same can also be said for other kinds of losses, such as the loss of our health, our youth, a role or passion. Inevitably, we experience feelings of grief and loss when someone or something we have cared for, valued and had a close or important connection with is no longer part of our everyday life. When the person was someone we were particularly close to, when it was a career we had dedicated much time and energy to, or when we lose capacity due to accident or ill-health, a large part of our identity can be connected, knowingly or unknowingly, to that which we have lost. This means that when the relationship finishes, we are not only losing that person or role, but also possibly a part of our identity. Our future plans, other relationships relating to that person, how we lived our everyday life, our sense of purpose and reasons for being, can all be affected. When we lose someone traumatically, this kind of loss can be amplified in a profound way. Even when we've long known someone was unwell and would eventually leave, the loss can still take us by surprise. Known losses can still come as a hard shock.

Whilst we may intellectually understand profound grief, and have great empathy for it, experiencing it is often a very different thing. Grief is not something we often discuss in Western society, and this may be to our detriment as it can leave us unprepared and unaware of how to navigate it and care well for ourselves or others through it. This can lead to people being so overwhelmed they may shut down, withdraw, and suppress their feelings due to the confusion and intensity of what they are trying to deal with, and not knowing how to manage it. What's normal? What's concerning? Who can we speak with without fear we'll distress them? Kindness and accountability matter as much in grief as they do in our relationships with those still here. Being kind to ourselves and finding the courage to sit, as gently as possible, with our grief feelings is a hard yet important part of how we approach loss. Knowing that the responsibility of feeling these feelings is ours alone to bear can feel overwhelming. As much as others might wish they could take our feelings away, sadly they are ours to process, but that doesn't mean we don't ask for help. It doesn't mean we don't talk to others about what is happening, it doesn't mean we can't be held and supported by those who are still here to care for us. Our accountability comes in understanding that there is only one way to move through grief, and that is to do the work of learning to cope with those feelings,

9. For a Reason, for a Season, for Life.

reaching out to those we can trust, be they personal or professional relationships, and asking them to be with us as we do this work, so that we might find our way to live with them and discover how love and joy might soothe and accompany them.

At 35 years old, I lost my husband in a car crash, having lost our first child to miscarriage six weeks earlier. The intensity of the pain that took up residence in my heart left me breathless, desperate, and immobilised in a state of shock and trauma. In time, I also came to see that I wasn't only grieving my family; I was grieving how much of myself had been bound to our relationship. I had not been aware of how deeply my identity was connected to my husband, the hope of our child and our shared future. The power of this grief also began to impact another large part of my identity, my vocation as a psychologist. At the time, I couldn't imagine ever being able to undertake my job as a therapist again, not when I felt such raw, powerful pain. I could not see how I could sit with others and risk them feeling the depth of my pain when they had come with their own.

To begin with, I didn't know why I got up every day, if it was not to create a life and family with my husband, if it wasn't to discover the world together and build our business, why was I here if not for that? I recall standing, staring out of the lounge room window at the outside world, everything was so still, there wasn't a breath of wind. It was as if the hills and lake that stretched before me were as frozen in time as my heart felt. I remained there not knowing what my place was in the world, and why I was in it anymore. My identity had been profoundly related to my marriage, and yet I did not have a clue that it was so inextricably linked until it wasn't.

My supervisor, who was supporting me in this space of

loss, gently told me that we heal by living again. Living again looked tricky without a clear identity to work from. That left me with one option, I had to formulate a new identity, one that took the threads of who I used to be and blended them with who I was now, and who I intended to become. It was a very slow process and took many years for me to weave those threads into something tangible that gave me comfort, purpose, and a way to feel safe being present. There is no rushing grief; it takes the time it takes.

After 25 years of working with people, I have come to believe that we heal with grief, not from it. Because grief eventually becomes an integral part of our daily experience. It may pop up more intensely from time to time and, at others, rest peacefully within. It becomes part of our identity in a positive way, if we allow it, symbolising something special we shared with someone—or, if the loss is of a role, career, or ability, symbolising our skills, achievements and dedication.

When we lose key people or roles in our lives that form a central part of our world, we are not always immediately aware of just how integral they are to our sense of identity. It might be a little bit of a cliché to say you don't know what you have until you lose it, but it can be disarmingly true. People who lose their health may often reflect on this too. But this also rings true for people who lose their careers or passions. The loss of a major part of our life can leave us with no idea of who we now are, or what we are to do instead. The loss of our vocation or calling, be it through injury or circumstance, can be deeply distressing and full of grief. In these moments, we can feel very vulnerable. This is when kindness and accountability for both ourselves, and given to us by others, can make all the difference.

9. For a Reason, for a Season, for Life.

I recall listening to a gentleman on a podcast discuss grief and, for me, he encapsulated it perfectly when he said he just wanted a T-shirt saying, "please be gentle with me; I'm grieving". Not because he wanted to gain sympathy or have others feel sorry for him, and not to play the victim or gain favours. But to signal to others to be kind, careful, and a little extra considerate in this difficult time. People can wear masks with their grief because it is a very private experience and those dealing with the high intensity of loss may not wish to have others feel their pain and suffer by proxy. So, they hold the mask in place to navigate daily life. But in private, they feel the wracking loss, leaving them with little capacity to cope with anything else.

Managing grief, no matter how it comes to you, is a task you are likely to have to undertake. If you try to suppress it or divert it, unfortunately, it may create more problems for you. There's only one way through grief, and that is to do the work. Not long after the police had informed me about the loss of my husband, I distinctly heard my own mind saying, "Can I fast forward to the part where I'm OK?" Being a psychologist with years of experience, I was aware of the long journey that lay ahead of me. Knowing how much I loved my husband, I was fully aware of the depth of pain that was also ahead of me. But beyond this, I somehow knew that one day I would be able to say that I was OK and mean it.

If you are experiencing grief and loss, be kind to yourself and give yourself the gentleness and grace of time to sit with it. It isn't pretty. It isn't easy. But when you embrace the whole spectrum of grief, you don't only find the raw and the painful; you can find the beautiful and the expansive as well. There is peace in grief. If you allow it, it can touch your heart and open you up to appreciate things in ways others, who have not had such a loss, do not experience. Sometimes in grief our senses become heightened, and we experience things more intensely and positively, where smells, tastes, and touch all feel amplified and more vibrant and beautiful. This may be available only briefly, and allowing yourself to be fully present—though hard—can help. It can be an incredible and enriching experience. **Where there is loss, there is a chance for discovery.**

When you let go of one thing, it leaves a space. This means there is then room for something new to move in. Whether you have lost a friend, a family member, a partner, your health, or a role or passion, you have had, in that now vacant space, there may come experiences you would have never known otherwise. Perhaps you might discover a depth of joy previously unimagined or connections that teach you more about who you are. This isn't to say, of course, that the person or role you lost is replaceable or that any one person or relationship or way of being is better than another. They are merely different and open the possibility of new experiences. There is no rush to put anything in that space. You decide when something new is able to come into your life; no one else does. When you can embrace this space and welcome something new in, your grief may lessen. But do it in your own time.

There are some small things that may help support you as you move through the grief and loss cycle, anchor points that might help you feel more grounded when you feel untethered from yourself. Looking after the basics is a good first step, making sure you are eating regularly, even if it is only a little. Allow yourself to be guided instinctually by what might bring comfort to your body. Mindfully balancing your diet as much as you can, so that it does not include too much junk food or comfort food that could cause you other problems later. Make sure you rest. Sleep may be an issue for some time when grieving, but at least by resting your body you can recoup some energy. Drinking plenty of water to keep hydrated and maybe consider that when dealing with loss you avoid alcohol/drugs, as this may hinder the process of feeling your feelings, as it could numb them too much. You are likely to have to deal with your feelings eventually; sometimes it might be best to just get into them. Movement, whether it is exercise, dance, yoga, walking, or something else, may aid you in transmuting these emotional experiences and help you to connect back to yourself. This may aid you in learning how to be this new version of you in the present. Movement can provide a remarkable bridge for focus, as you concentrate on the motions your mind is absorbed and the mental gymnastics can settle down, and with that movement can come the sense of change, with the good hormones produced by exercise supporting you along the way.

    A good second step, and perhaps the most supportive of all, is to start building new memories. Do activities alone or with others and start creating a catalogue of new experiences. It may be hard at first because you might be missing what you have lost, but with conscious awareness that it is ok to carry on, to live and enjoy things still, this may slowly start to shift. This can give your brain new memories to focus on, ones that hopefully bring you joy and laughter, so that, in time, you might have created enough of them that they allow the painful feelings of loss to be soothed, and the memories of what was lost to be experienced in a more peaceful and positive way, not with such intense longing, but with appreciation for having had it. If your mind has other options to choose from, hopefully it can pick the lighter and brighter new memories and help support you in seeing that whilst there is loss, there is still life.

Grief is one of those companions that does not necessarily leave you. There may still be moments, maybe years in the future, that you might miss and feel the loss of that person who was in your life, or you recall that way you lived, that career you were passionate about. You might think of that person or life every day. That's OK too. You are allowed to have those feelings and thoughts. Honour them and be with them. Judging yourself negatively is an emotional energy you don't need to add into the situation. Just be mindful that if you do think of this person or this way of life often, that you do so from a place of gratitude and acceptance that this time has now ended and new ways of being can bring different joys and pleasures, and be as equally valuable. Living from the past and trying to alter your present reality to get it back may not serve you; this is one of those not so easy parts of grief, the whole letting go thing. Remember, letting go does not mean you lose the memories or feelings that were shared; you simply open a bigger space for something else beautiful and great to come in as well.

If you have learnt to live again and reformed your identity to be about more than your relationships or a way of life, but to also be about the relationship you have with yourself, then those moments of missing and of loss may become briefer and less intense. You may learn to live with your grief and make it a positive part of your life. One day, you might be able to see your grief as an old friend, one that can remind you of some of the special and brilliant parts of your life that you were able to live. Our tears honour the truth of what we feel and what we have experienced. They say what our words cannot express. They need not be feared or judged harshly.

Almost nothing on this planet lasts forever, except the

experience of love. It can visit us in countless forms: through individuals, families, friends, careers, passions, animals, and even our love of nature. When we allow ourselves to stay open and adapt to how love may appear, it can then feel eternal. This includes the love we cultivate for ourselves. Self-love allows us to give love—and to receive it from others and the world around us.

You are always going to be the one person who gets up for you each day. You are always going to be the one person who can have your own back. You are always going to be the one person you can travel halfway around the world from and still not escape. You may as well make peace with being you and do your best to love and care for yourself in the most sustainable ways possible.

When you can adapt to love being transmuted through different mediums, different people, and different experiences; this can support you in being kind to yourself, care for yourself well and, just as importantly, do the same for others. **Love is diverse: adapt, and love adapts with you—and, in this way, it becomes sustainable. Remember, loving yourself means supporting yourself to be you.**

Exercise: "Dear Me ...Revisited"

If you read Book 1 – The Subtle Injury of Influence, you may have completed one of the first exercises and written a letter to yourself. If you wrote to yourself, go and find this letter and now, reread it and then using all that you have learned about yourself and considering the things you have decided to work on or improve, write yourself a reply.

Write a letter back to the person you were. Perhaps, you offer kindness and understanding. Show yourself compassion and express how you now wish to take better care of yourself.

If you did not complete this exercise previously, then simply write a letter to yourself, addressing who you were, who you are now, and who you wish to continue to be using the self-knowledge you have gained from reading the Books in the Adaptable Sustainable Psychology collection.

You might only write a few lines, or it could turn into a page or two. The amount you write is not important; the content is what will be meaningful. There is no right or wrong way to do this exercise.

Be mindful of any negative self-judgment that might arise. If this exercise doesn't look or feel the way you think it "should," choose to be kind to yourself instead.

9. For a Reason, for a Season, for Life.

To begin:

- Sit down in a quiet, private place where you are unlikely to be disturbed.
- Turn off your phone and free yourself as much as possible from external distractions.
- Using pen and paper (which is preferable to typing on a device), begin writing a letter to yourself.

In your letter, consider expressing:

- How you see yourself now and how you wish to be in the future.
- How you look after yourself currently in terms of self-care and what you want to start or maintain.
- What it feels like to be you and what has changed, what you would like to keep working on.
- What you value most about being you.

If you find this exercise brings up difficult emotions, please pause and consider seeking support from a therapist or mental health professional.

The Adaptable Sustainable Psychology Collection: Book 4

Pause — Reflect — Landscape

1. **Pause** - Take a moment to sit with what you have just learned and consider it.

- The loss of relationships, people, our health and our careers can take a heavy toll on us and leave us with a space where a large part of our identity may have been, often without us necessarily realising just how much of ourselves was tied into what we lost.
- In grief we can support ourselves through offering kindness towards ourselves and seeking it from others and being accountable in doing the work of grief gently and from a place of courage, asking for help along the way.
- We can look to start the healing of our grief by learning to live again, but when so much of our identity is missing, this can be challenging and it might feel overwhelming.
- In grief, it is not just the loss of whatever is no longer part of our life that causes us pain and discomfort, it is also the loss of whatever part of ourselves was experienced through that relationship, person, career or capacity.
- Being extra gentle and compassionate with ourselves when we are grieving and adjusting to loss is important. Doing the work of dealing with grief is valid, as

9. For a Reason, for a Season, for Life.

    suppressing it can cause further harm, ignoring or denying its impacts may create other issues for us to cope with.

- Defining our own grief path, at our own pace and in our own time may help us regain a small fraction of the sense of control that the loss has taken away from us.
- Grief is a spectrum that offers us opportunities to honour what we had and experience the profound loss of this, but it can also open a space of appreciation, gratitude and awareness for what is, what we had, and what might now come into our lives. We can move between great peace and great pain, and tenderness is required at both ends of the spectrum.
- Looking after the basics can help when grieving, such as resting the body as much as possible if we cannot sleep, eating something, staying hydrated, avoiding drugs and alcohol, exercising or moving, and being outside with nature whenever possible may all help us with the process.
- Starting to create new memories may help give our minds somewhere else to land and other things to focus on, and support the belief there is life beyond the loss.
- Embracing our tears and allowing ourselves to build a new relationship with ourselves and our evolving identity is all part of the grief work and can help us unite who we were with who we are now, and who we might become.
- When we embrace the idea of self-love, it may open the possibility to receive love from others, even after loss.
- Self-love can be a hard journey at times, yet when based in acceptance, humility and gratitude you can truly find ways to support yourself in being OK to be you.

2. **Reflect** - Answer the following questions:

- Have you spent much time in your life discussing grief and loss? Is this a part of your culture or your society that can help prepare you for when these times come?
- Do you think it might be beneficial to talk more openly about the journey that comes with the loss of someone or something important to us?

3. **Landscape** - Step back from the details and see how this new information fits in with the bigger picture of your life. Consider your history, what is going on for you now, who and what is in your life, and the future you want for yourself.

- ✓ What has influenced your understanding of grief and your attitude towards loss? Do you see this as being potentially helpful for you in the event of either unexpected or expected loss?
- ✓ Is there anything you could work toward changing or seek to evolve within yourself that might make things that bit easier and more bearable should you have to deal with loss? What do you think could help you to prepare for this?
- ✓ Have you experienced a loss that has been hard for you to sit with and heal from? Is this something you may want some professional support with to be able to move into a new phase of your life, or do you have people you trust that you can open up to and ask for help?

10. Review of Insights into You

Investing time and energy in understanding what kinds of relationships suit us—what behaviours and values align with us, and what helps us be our best—can pay off. As we learn to care for ourselves, we build compassion, own what's ours, and recognize what isn't. From this place of feeling "good enough" and practicing appropriate self-care, it becomes easier to get more from our relationships—and do the kinds of growth we can't achieve alone. When both people move to the rhythm of kindness and accountability, the dance of the relationship flows more smoothly.

Managing our stress well, whether it's making sure we have enough of the good kind of stress or minimising the amount of distress we are exposed to, may help us maintain and manage relationships more efficiently and effectively. Working out when we can either deflect or displace to reduce stress to help lighten our load can be an effective tool for assisting us in limiting our stress to ensure we can maximise our relationship potential.

The relationship map we carry in our minds often doesn't match reality. When the map is not giving us clear directions or taking us down a path that we cannot traverse together this could lead to problems, arguments, and disengagement occurring in the relationship. It can help to examine our expectations and assumptions—where they came from, whether they are fair, and whether they support healthy connection. Heavy online communication can influence or erode real world skills, and this could leave others feeling misunderstood, unheard or unseen. Paying close attention, listening actively, and leading with compassion can strengthen relationships. When we know what works for us (and what doesn't), understand our expectations, and feel comfortable being ourselves, we can build personal agency, which, in turn, may support us in staying present, making careful choices, and drawing a more accurate map for relationships that truly fit who we are and who we are with.

How we interact and engage with responsibility can be affected by our past experiences and how other people around us manage their responsibility. Paying attention to how we are showing up when it comes to being responsible might help protect both ourselves and others from harm. Identifying if we have tendencies to be overly-responsible, under-responsible, irresponsible, or personally responsible, may help us become aware of potential consequences from our actions or inaction that we might benefit from addressing. When responsibility is approached from a place of self-acceptance, growth can be generated and used as a platform for change.

Building trust in ourselves forms an important part of the foundation for being able to take accountability and move into a place of personal responsibility. Trauma can affect how we engage with and relate to responsibility, becoming compassionately aware of this and managing it either with professional help or through our own appropriate self-care may assist us in generating trust with ourselves again, and could increase our chances of making trusting connections with others.

10. Review of Insights into You

Over-relying on justification can be a barrier to self-trust, as can being unable to forgive ourselves and others. Forgiveness is a difficult area to discuss, but learning to forgive ourselves or release painful moments of our past is another part of our journey to finding inner peace and may ease the path to feeling comfortable to be ourselves and facilitate healthy relationships.

People can fight over power in relationships, especially when they are feeling powerless in other areas of their lives. Understanding how we are sitting with our sense of power and control and being able to assess other people's position, may help create more constructive communication and enable connections, rather than becoming a grab for power. Recognising where our or the other person's self-worth sits is a helpful marker for indicating where power plays might appear in a relationship and potentially be used to manipulate and control. Managing our sense of worth can support healthy connections and may insulate us from being taken advantage of. Seeking out circular relationships, where everyone regards each other's needs as equally important as their own, may lead to greater appreciation, compassion and understanding amongst one another.

Communication is about the transfer of information and communion is the spiritual, emotional, and mental connection where we can share ideas, thoughts and feelings. There are many things that can affect our communication and potential for communion. These include not being fully present, using negative speech or trying to cause harm to another, using silence as a mechanism for control, or being triggered by a painful past that can either lead to dissociation or generate misunderstandings due to the high activation and overwhelm from emotional reactivity. Practicing our communication and being aware of what elements can go wrong for us may help us improve and maintain our skills and lead to healthier and happier relationships.

Accepting ourselves for who we are may help support us in being able to live peacefully with one another and grow together. Ensuring our expectations are not getting in the way of self-acceptance, and that we can create pathways to gratitude and humility, may lead to us developing a kindlier attitude towards ourselves and others. Through self-acceptance we may support our capacity to see our own and other's intentions. By becoming clear about our intentions, especially when communicating with others, we may be able to avoid or de-escalate arguments. Taking time to understand our deeper intentions, which may not always be obvious, and ascertaining the intentions of other people can lead to discussing matters more openly, fostering greater appreciation and understanding of one another. This can then lead us towards being able to work together co-operatively and effectively.

Loss of any kind can be deeply challenging and difficult for us. It may affect our sense of identity and our place in the world. Being mindful and gentle of what we are dealing with in a space of grief can support us on the journey towards healing. We can help heal grief by living again and creating a new identity, based on who we have been, who we are now, and who we would like to move towards being, opening the space for new opportunities that might not have been previously available to us. Taking care of the basics like resting, eating, staying hydrated, avoiding drugs and alcohol, moving and making time to build new, beautiful memories can all help us on that long and difficult journey that grief takes us on. Being aware that grief is a spectrum that can move from the very painful to the intensely peaceful can help counterbalance the work of grief. Focusing on compassion and self-care can encourage us to softly, and at our own pace, find our way back to ourselves and back to the world again. Love adapts, and then it sustains—and from a place of acceptance and being content to be ourselves, we may actualise self-love.

Exercise: Insights Gained into Yourself

In seeking to create healthy relationships, learning to be kind to ourselves and being able to accept accountability by raising our self-worth, caring for our emotional wounds, managing our vulnerabilities and feeling good enough, all may be of assistance. Doing this inner work may help support us in being able to offer the very same kindness and accountability to others. Good communication can create communion. And from communion intimacy, deep connection, and trust may grow.

Looking back over your notes and the exercises that you have done in this book, take a moment to write down your answers to the following questions. Reflect on what this work has shown you and be OK if it is not always comfortable. As you have, by now, learned, there may be something you can do about that.

1. Do you know what you want to experience in a relationship? What can uplift and affirm you? What kind of relationship environment can support you into being the best version of yourself and help you provide the same support to another?

2. What are your signs of too much distress and not enough good stress? In what ways could you self-limit your stress, knowing what kind of person you are and

your vulnerabilities? Which areas of your life could use deflection or displacement tools?

3. Do you fear growth in relationships? Do you walk away from relationship challenges? Do you stay too long with people who do not grow? What kind of relationship do you thrive in?

4. What have you learnt about your assumptions and expectations of relationships? What can you do to manage your expectations to be a more responsive communicator? Do you have assumptions about others that can create misunderstandings or might be unfair?

5. Are you managing your responsibility in a balanced way, or do you fear holding responsibility? Do you have relationships where you are over-responsible? Do you have relationships where you are under-responsible, or irresponsible? What would being personally responsible look like for you?

6. Have you developed a deep sense of self-trust? Is this something you would like to work on more consciously? What—or who—can you let go of that could allow you to release any unnecessary pain from the past? Do you struggle with self-forgiveness or letting things go? Which exercises from Books 1-3 could help you with this?

7. Are there ways in which you can improve your communication style? Are you letting the need for power affect your relationships? Do you consider the needs of others as equal to your own? What could open up the pathway to being able to transition from communication to communion?

8. Are you someone who practices gratitude each day and pays compliments to others? How could you maintain a practice of gratitude as often as possible? Could this be an inner conversation with yourself about what you are grateful for? Have you tried journalling to show yourself what kind of language you use, observe how you speak with others, and review this information to see how you tell your stories? Is it from a problem-focused perspective, a solution-focused perspective, or a gratitude-focused perspective?

9. Have you found any expectations about yourself or others that could block self-acceptance? Are you someone who practices humility, or is this a skill you might benefit from acquiring? Do you have a clear connection to understanding what your intentions are? Can you accurately assess or ask others comfortably what their intentions are? Are you honest with yourself about your intentions? Can you communicate these fairly and respectfully with others?

10. If you have experienced loss or recognise you may one day have a significant loss, are grieving, or worry about loss happening, gently ask yourself what might support you to get through such times? What things might bring a ray of light? How can you make sure you take care of your basics, like eating regularly (even if only a little), drinking water, resting, and doing some kind of movement or exercise? What could bring you comfort and help rebuild trust in yourself? Who could be a support to you in these times, personally or professionally?

11. Adaptable Sustainable Psychology: Principals and Ways of Being

As children entering the world and adults living out our lives, it can feel like a vision is given to us of who we are supposed to be and how others need us to be. We may continue this journey without opportunity or encouragement to make a conscious choice about **who _we_ want to be** so that we can truly thrive. Thus, we may end up living through a vision of ourselves not necessarily borne out of our own insights, but influenced by experiences, media and other people.

If we are shown how to access insights into who we are and then use these to inform the vision of who we wish to be, then our experience of life may change quite drastically.

Exploring what an Adaptable Sustainable Psychology (ASP) way of life could look like, we suggest it involves:

1. Choosing a way of being that is unique to you and supports you to adapt and thrive in ever-changing environments.

2. Developing a considered, compassionate mindset that recognises what you've been through and how culture,

the media or people may have shaped you—sometimes creating internal beliefs that don't serve you well.

3. Learning to change and influence your life by altering unhelpful beliefs, adjusting unsustainable coping methods, building self-trust, and becoming more comfortable with discomfort.

4. Building a framework that supports a safe space to experience and release feelings, freeing you from emotional burdens that do not serve you.

5. Cultivating awareness of when to focus on yourself and when to forget yourself, sustaining growth through an evolving capacity to perceive what benefits you and others.

This way of life may support you in being resilient, vulnerable, and accountable and, above all, compassionate.

To cultivate and live through an Adaptable Sustainable Psychology means to:

- Act compassionately towards yourself and other people in all things.

- Balance self-focus with self-forgetting. Consider and manage your needs with the needs of others. Care well for yourself so you can care well for others. Actively manage responsibility—own your part and allow others to hold accountability for theirs.

- Know yourself well and manage yourself well. Recognise what works (and what doesn't) and, when required, self-adjust. Be personally accountable for your expectations and actions; they belong to you.

- Support mental wellbeing and building emotional sustainability by recognising, understanding, and then readjusting any damaging beliefs and behaviours that could influence your life in unhelpful ways. Use committed practice to adapt beliefs as you or circumstances change, creating opportunities to make the best of your life and of being you.

- Find your way to being OK with who you are at any given point in time. Respect and accept yourself as you are, and offer the same to others.

- Learn to trust in your capacity to cope when you are very much not OK. Learn how to be as comfortable as possible, especially when you are uncomfortable. Actively coach, support, and nurture yourself as you would someone you care for, such as a child.

- Be clear on which coping strategies are sustainable for managing your emotions—and which may cause problems either now or later.

- Allow acceptance to guide you to surrender and let go of what you cannot change. Release old hurts or forgive your errors to support moving forward and finding new opportunities. Develop a mindset of self-trust, and know that, whatever occurs, you can find a safe way to cope and make the best of the situation.

- Immerse yourself in the joy of giving to others and working collectively to uplift one another. Be willing to let go of relationships that are not kind, fair, respectful or do not align with you. Acknowledge that one-way streets in relationships often don't necessarily last.

- Communicate and commune by being clear about your intentions and by seeking to understand others' intentions. Be a careful communicator: pause, fully assess the situation, and respond after considering your context and history, while remaining curious about the other person's.

- Foster relationships where you treat each other with equal kindness. Be clear about your boundaries and discuss them openly. Trust yourself to meet your needs as you move through life, until new opportunities come along.

- Check in with yourself to know you are enough. Check your accountability to be sure that you have done enough. Learn to trust that you have enough—and check that you're not burning yourself out unnecessarily.

Final Words

Well done on making it this far. As you've learned, the journey doesn't end here. You can spend a lifetime caring for yourself, managing how you relate to others, and tending to your relationships—work that evolves over time. Other forms of healing may help along the way, including professionals, guides, courses, books, or therapy. For now, take a moment to acknowledge and congratulate yourself for the work you have done.

Be kind to yourself about the insights you've gained, and be compassionate in how you use them to guide and support yourself towards what you seek.

It takes courage to face ourselves. Perhaps add that quality to what you know about yourself—if you haven't already realised it.

Final Exercise: Where Your Insights Inform Your Vision

This final exercise invites you to bring together insights from all four Books: who you are, what helps and what no longer serves you, how you cope with stress and pain (and whether those coping methods are adaptable and sustainable), how you relate to and consider others, and how all of this makes you feel to be you.

You'll now use this information to clarify a vision for how you want to move through life—caring for yourself and for others.

Sometimes, we need to see it to be it.
Sometimes, we need to feel it to create it.
Sometimes, we need to seek it to understand it.
Sometimes, we need to share it to appreciate it.

This exercise may help you shape a vision of who you are, how you cope, and how you treat yourself and others. Gather all the notes, exercises, and insights you've accumulated from any or all of the Books, find a calm, safe, quiet space, and lean into whatever supports your mental wellbeing and builds your emotional sustainability.

- Maybe write out the type of person you would like to be. Include how this version of you handles difficult situations. What would you say to yourself to nurture and

Final Words

encourage yourself through hard times? How do you treat yourself and others? What helps you thrive in better times? Cope with and endure the tougher ones? What attitude do you want towards your self-care and the care of others? Imagine the best version of you in both challenging and wonderful moments.

- You might express this as a metaphor, a poem, or as a story.
- Or create a drawing or collage that represents how you intend to feel and be.
- You could look to generate a bodily sense of what it may feel like once you've made these changes and are using them every day, and practice being present with these feelings.
- You might visualise yourself as something in nature you admire—say, a deep lake: the surface may ripple and currents may move below, but at the very bottom everything remains calm, still, and steady.
- You could imagine yourself at 80-years-old, looking back. What do you want to see? What have you done that leaves you content and satisfied? What kind of person have you been? How have you treated yourself and others? Did you support yourself, reach for your dreams, and encourage others to pursue theirs?

Using your creativity or analytical mind, draw on what you've learned so your vision of yourself is informed by your own insight—and make sure it's a vision you feel comfortable with.

If this exercise brings up difficult emotions, consider pausing and seeking support from a suitably qualified health professional.

Acknowledgments - With Gratitude

I would like to respectfully acknowledge and thank all the individuals who have inspired, created, and contributed to our current body of psychological knowledge. This book draws on the brilliant work of many who have postulated theories, tested them, or created therapeutic techniques to help those in distress.

My deepest thanks go to every client I've had the privilege of working with. Each interaction has been a valuable learning experience, teaching me more about how humans are shaped by one another and the world around them.

I would like to thank my parents, who have provided a backdrop of consistent support. I am deeply fortunate and blessed to have been inspired by my mother's constant capacity for forgiveness and care, and by my father's determination to keep moving forward, no matter the obstacles.

I'm incredibly grateful to my dedicated, kind, hard-working, and funny partner, Andy. Knowing his love and support is there as a constant, and receiving his encouragement when things have been difficult, has made an enormous difference over the past few years.

To all my friends, thank you—particularly Talina, who has never doubted me and has been a steady stream of support, encouragement, and kindness. I'm also super grateful for my long-term school friends Kerry, Katie, and Laura, whose wisdom, humour, and compassion carry me through life's challenges. And to Jim, whose company has been one of the greatest blessings—offering nourishment, fun, learning, and the simple joy of sharing life.

I would like to express my gratitude and respect to my mentor and supervisor, Dr. Bruce Wilson, for his care and guidance over the years; to Helen and Alex for their generosity, intelligence, and skills in promoting this work; and to Kerry for her editing talents, positive support, and insightful guidance.

I'm extremely thankful to everyone at Author Services Australia who helped bring this book to life. Regardless of the outcome, I'm truly pleased with what we've created - thanks in large part to the brilliant, patient, and hard-working individuals who put up with my endless list of revisions.

My final acknowledgment goes to my first husband. While I lost you on the 12th day of the 12th month in 2012 – a day where so much of my world ended - I have from that awful moment been continually supported by the love we shared, the hope you gave me, and your constant belief in what I could achieve. I would not be who I am without you.

www.ingramcontent.com/pod-product-compliance
Lightning Source LLC
Chambersburg PA
CBHW061727070526
44583CB00024B/3043